A 30 DAY RETREAT

A Personal Guide to Spiritual Renewal

WILLIAM C. MILLS

PAULIST PRESS
New York/Mahwah, NJ

Cover design by Joy Taylor
Book design by Lynn Else

Library of Congress Cataloging-in-Publication Data

Mills, William C.
    A 30 day retreat : a personal guide to spiritual renewal / William C. Mills.
      p. cm.
    Distinctive title: A thirty day retreat
    ISBN 978-0-8091-4642-0 (alk. paper)
    1. Bible. N.T.—Meditations. 2. Spiritual retreats—Catholic Church. I. Title.
II. Title: A thirty day retreat.
    BS2341.55.M56 2010
    242'.5—dc22

                                                        2009047950

Published by Paulist Press
997 Macarthur Boulevard
Mahwah, New Jersey 07430

www.paulistpress.com

Printed and bound in the
United States of America

Contents

For
Father Paul N. Tarazi
with Thanksgiving

"If we walk in the light as he himself is in the light, we have fellowship with one another." (1 John 1:7)

Introduction

As a pastor of a small congregation in a metropolitan city, and as a teacher of courses on the Bible at a local university, I have encountered many people who are seeking a meaningful spiritual life. Whether young or old, married or single, with children or without, people want spirituality that is uplifting and comforting, as well as challenging and enlightening. They seek sound teachings that will feed and sustain them along their life journey. They expect substance for the long haul. They want content that will help them live through difficult moments in life, such as sickness and death, transitions in job and home, and tragic events in the world, such as terrorism, war, and poverty.

Furthermore, people are asking what I call *the hard questions* pertaining to the meaning of life: How can I live out my faith in both the world and the workplace? How can I remain faithful to the many commitments in life, including family, work, school, and Church? What does it mean to have a vocation? What does the Lord expect of me in the here and now? And the big one: Will I ever make it to heaven?

Where can people find such answers to these questions? Some turn to the mass media and others to friends or family who might offer some spiritual insight. Others turn to nature or to New Age religion or to self-help books. However, many people, especially Christians, turn to the Bible. The Bible is full of spiritual wisdom and insight that transcends time and space, culture and geography, gender and race. The very fact that the Word of God has been translated into more than a thousand different languages and is still one of the best-selling books of all time testifies to its importance for the spiritual life. The Bible is not just words *about* God, but the very Word *of* God, which has been perfectly revealed to us in his Son, Jesus Christ; "The Word became flesh and dwelt among us, full of grace and truth; we have beheld his glory, glory as of the only Son from the Father" (John 1:14).

Yet people often get lost while reading the Bible. They are confused when encountering the strange names, places, themes, metaphors, and symbols that appear throughout its pages. Face it, how many friends do you have named Delilah, Methuselah, or Nebuchadnezzar? Not many, I am sure! People often get so frustrated that they close the Bible, never to open it again. This is quite unfortunate because the Bible offers us timeless guidance for our journey to the kingdom.

Yet there is hope. In *A 30 Day Retreat: A Personal Guide to Spiritual Renewal*, I share some insights about the spiritual journey with those of you who are on the same path. There is no way to learn everything; we are all pilgrims seeking God in everyday living, in the here and now. This book is a road map that guides and leads us to the still waters. As a pastor and professor, I envision my role as a tour guide, offering my knowledge and life experience in order to help others who are broken, hurt, and in need of direction. There is a lot of pain and sense of isolation in this world. Good tour guides knows their way around the town or city, passing on their many years of life knowledge to strangers who come and visit. However, it is up to the tourist to make sense of their trip and what they see: the sights and sounds, "smells and bells," so to speak.

Spirituality cannot be developed overnight; it takes time. I like to describe the spiritual journey as a marathon. One of my good friends, who is also a pastor, runs at least one marathon a year. One day I asked him what is involved in running in such a race. Every day he leaves his church office at 2 p.m. and, after time for warming up and stretching, he runs for three hours. He does this six days a week. He runs, even though he might not be feeling well. He *has* to run, even though he might not be in the mood for running. Training for a marathon requires diligence and dedication. Then, of course there is the high-calorie, low-fat diet and gallons of extra water for hydration to keep him healthy. This is his routine for most of the year.

As you can see, running a marathon requires dedication, careful planning, and lots of practice. He said that it is impossible to run twenty-six miles without putting in the extra time; a runner would never finish the race. So as with our spiritual life: we cannot reach the end if we expect quick results. Our life is not a quick spring, a few seconds, and then it is over. Following Jesus also takes a lot of time, patience, dedication, and careful planning. Even the Apostle Paul likens the spiritual journey with running: "Let us run with perseverance the race that is set before us, looking to Jesus the pioneer and perfecter of our faith"

(Heb 12:1). Hopefully this book is a small step in the right direction in our common journey together in Christ.

In these pages you will find thirty, easy-to-read meditations on key passages of the Bible that I have personally found meaningful in my own journey. The chapters focus on such topics as forgiveness, love, repentance, vocation, and discipleship, as well as others. The easy-to-read format allows readers to take one chapter per day in order to deepen and further reflect on the Word of God. Each chapter concludes with a short section called *Food for Thought* that includes several questions or statements that will assist you in exploring the specific themes of each chapter.

This book can be used as a resource for both personal devotion and small group discussions. Readers are encouraged to use it in conjunction with the journaling process so that you will return to this book again and again for spiritual inspiration and encouragement. The spiritual journey is not an easy one. We need as much help as we can get; we certainly cannot do it alone. Jesus sent out even his disciples two by two into the mission field: Paul traveled with Barnabas, Silas, and Timothy. Many of the great saints and spiritual leaders of the Christian tradition also had spiritual companions or friends that helped them along the way—Frances and Claire, John of the Cross and Teresa of Avila, among others. Fellow pilgrims and travelers have unearthed pearls of wisdom in the pages of scripture. Hopefully we can mine those same pages for the same wisdom and insight that God gives us.

How to Use This Book

A 30 Day Retreat is designed either for personal spiritual devotion or for a small group retreat or discussion. A retreat is time away from everyday living, in which we can relax, rejuvenate ourselves, and reassess our life. It is a time for focused introspection, prayer, and discernment. Some people go on a retreat for a specific purpose, such as dealing with a recent loss or death in their life. Others go on retreats for discerning a change in vocation or a major life transition, such as divorce or home relocation. Nevertheless, a retreat requires that the person remain open to the Holy Spirit. It is a time to slow down a little, away from the many distractions that get between us and God.

Before reading this book, try to take some quiet time away from the regular hustle and bustle of everyday life. This is not always easy, because we are under a constant barrage of e-mails, phone calls, and faxes, not to mention the background noise of everyday living, television, radio, and the routine of home life. I ask that you literally spend time away in peaceful silence, away from the noise of the world. Find a quiet spot in your house such as a home office, back porch, or perhaps in a quiet place in a park. If you are in a small group setting, the group might want to meet in a parish meeting room or in the sanctuary. The group may want to look into meeting at a local retreat house or monastery, which, of course, would be an ideal setting.

Whether you are by yourself or in a small group, you will need to take this book as well as a Bible translation that you will feel comfortable reading. You might also want to bring along a diary or journal. I always find that when I am on retreat, many thoughts come to me throughout the day, and I like to write them down for future reference. We cannot always trust our failing memories! Some people like to write in a spiritual journal as a regular spiritual practice, a process that helps them engage their inner thoughts, temptations, fears, and dreams. *A 30 Day Retreat* will serve as an excellent resource for the journaling process as well.

Before you begin, take a few moments to quiet your mind and your heart. It is senseless to read scripture when your mind is going a mile a minute, worrying about shopping, cooking dinner, and other countless household chores. Some people like to use a mantra to assist them to quiet down their mind, such as repeating the name Jesus. A friend of mine shared this particular saying with me: "Let us remember that we are in the holy presence of God." This saying has remained with me for a long time. I use it often when I want to quiet down my mind and heart. You will find your own way to quiet your mind.

Next, take a few deep breaths. As you exhale, let all your worries and problems leave you. Throughout the day we collect so much "toxic waste" in the form of useless information, thoughts, fantasies, and the like, that it blocks the Spirit from working in us. Letting these things go before reading the Bible is a good way to deep-clean our mind.

When you feel that you are quiet and rested, open this book and read the scripture verses that begin the chapter. You might also want to read the same scripture passages in the Bible itself. After you are finished reading the scripture passage, take some time to let the words sink into your heart. Savor each word as if you were eating a delicious meal. Then, after you reflect on the words, you might want to ask yourself the following question: What are some of the feelings or emotions that you had when reading the passage? Depending on our mental state or the time of day, the scriptures speak to us differently.

While reading, you might want to ask yourself: What is God saying in this passage? We need to remember that each passage of scripture has its own particular context. When Paul wrote the Letter to the Corinthians, it was directed at the fledgling church in Corinth. However, we still read this epistle today because Paul's letters speak to us in the here and now. So you might also want to ask yourself, what is God saying to me *today*? This is the Word of God that is directed to *me* in *my* particular time, space, and situation. If you are in a small group setting, you might want to think about how this passage speaks to the group.

Then, after reading the scripture selection, read the meditation that I have provided in the rest of the chapter. Does any particular word, phrase, image, or idea stand out in your mind? Are there key phrases or ideas that might be unfamiliar or strange to your ear? If you are in a small group setting, you could use these questions as background material for your discussion. I always find small group discussions very fruitful. Other people may have similar or different experiences or understandings of the images, words, or ideas in the book.

If you are alone, take a few moments and write down your thoughts in a journal or diary. When using a journal, you will be able to return to these thoughts later. When you are finished reading the meditation for that particular passage, you then can turn to the Food for Thought section that concludes each chapter. These brief, focused questions and statements will further assist the reader in being open to the Holy Spirit and to delve deeper into each chapter. Treat this section as additional food for the spiritual journey. Each section also includes additional scripture references for further reading and reflection. Take some extra time to read these passages as well.

Finally, end each session with a short period of prayer and silence. Reading the Word of God is a holy activity. It is difficult to read Paul's Epistle to the Romans and then begin cleaning the house. A short period of reentry into your normal routine is important and necessary. Again, quiet down your mind; recite your favorite mantra or prayer such as the Lord's Prayer. If you are in a small group setting, you might want to stand in a circle and hold hands while praying. This might seem a bit awkward at first, but it has been my experience that holding hands while praying can physically unite the group as they recite their common prayer to God.

It is suggested that if you are using this book alone you will devote at least thirty to forty-five minutes for each chapter, including the opening and closing prayer, reading the scripture and the meditations, and journaling. Of course, more time can be devoted to this process. For a small group discussion, it is suggested that the group takes at least sixty to ninety minutes per chapter.

Generally speaking, the more people in a group, the longer the discussion period.

A 30 Day Retreat: A Personal Guide to Spiritual Renewal will not solve all of your spiritual questions or provide you easy answers of faith; of course, no book will do that. However, I would hope that it puts you in touch with the scriptures as a means of spiritual growth and edification, not only for today, but also for the rest of your life. It will help the the Bible to become your longtime companion and your roadmap to the kingdom. You will return back to it again and again through the weeks and months to come.

DAY 1
Walking By Faith
HEBREWS 11:1–3

Now faith is the assurance of things hoped for, the conviction of things not seen. Indeed, by faith our ancestors received approval. By faith we understand that the worlds were prepared by the word of God, so that what is seen was made from things that are not visible.

So much of our life is bittersweet, marked by mixed blessings, by joy and sadness, celebration and anxiety. Take the Christmas holidays, for example. We eat and drink and exchange presents with one another. Perhaps we visit a cousin or an aunt whom we haven't seen in a while. However, very quickly these wonderful times often turn sour. Despite hours, even days of preparation, the turkey might end up overcooked or not cooked enough. A particular gift, chosen at great care and expense, might be received indifferently. A friend or family member who has had one-too-many drinks might begin acting rude. The holidays are times when people often get angry, upset, irritated, and stressed. We actually end up looking forward to December 26, to everyone going home, and even to getting back to work.

Weddings are similar. We get so excited about planning the big day where we will make a life commitment with our soul mate. We anticipate the joys of spending life together in a new home and hopefully starting a new family. However, this too turns sour as we have our first fight. We cry, stomp our feet, and slam doors. What happened to the joy of our wedding day? What happened to those bright smiling faces and those feelings of pure love as we gazed into each other's eyes? The beautiful wedding flowers seem to wilt as the difficulties of marriage present themselves. Life is certainly full of mixed blessings.

We also find ourselves in this predicament of mixed emotions in our life of faith. The opening reading from the Book of Hebrews begins by speaking about faith, which the author says is "the assurance of things hoped for" and "the conviction of things not seen." Faith is trust, specifically, trust in God. When we say we have faith, we mean that we put our trust in something. Faith is lived in people's lives. Further along in the passage, the author specifically names people who were faithful to God:

> *And what more should I say? For time would fail me to tell of Gideon, Barak, Samson, Jephthah, of David and Samuel and the prophets — who through faith conquered kingdoms, administered justice, obtained promises, shut the mouths of lions, quenched raging fire, escaped the edge of the sword, won strength out of weakness, became mighty in war, put foreign armies to flight. Women received their dead by resurrection. Others were tortured, refusing to accept release, in order to obtain a better resurrection.* (Heb 11:32–35)

The author mentions people from a long time ago who lived in places far away; their names may even sound strange to our modern ear. These great men and women are commended for their faith in God and their faith in the promise of a savior. They were strong people: kings, soldiers, patriarchs, prophets, and leaders. David, for example, united the Twelve Tribes of Israel into one kingdom. Abraham was the first patriarch, the father of all nations. Noah built the ark and helped save humanity and the animals during the great flood. All of the people in the scriptures have their own particular story of faith. One could also look to Moses, Joshua, Job, Peter, Paul, Jesus' mother Mary, or Timothy as further examples of people of faith. They all followed the Lord and obeyed his word, yet oftentimes they also faltered too. Paul began his life by persecuting the very person whom he later preached throughout the whole Roman Empire! Through trials and difficulties, these people retained their faith that the Almighty One would deliver them out of the hand of their enemies and from the evil of this world. The Christian tradition has also provided us with a host of saints who themselves are exemplars of faith: Francis and Claire, Augustine, Gregory the Great, John Chrysostom, Seraphim of Sarov, Edith Stein, Elizabeth Seton, and many others. They were bishops, prophets, teachers, religious teachers, lay leaders, and more.

Yet at the same time, we know that these people also doubted God's power. Sometimes they even fell into despair and hopelessness. Even though David was a strong king, he had his loyal army officer Uriah killed so that he could take Uriah's wife Bathsheba as his bride. They questioned God's actions and decisions. The prophet Jonah didn't want to preach in Nineveh so he fled to Tarshish. Jeremiah told God that he was too young to be a prophet. Peter, who is known as the chief disciple, nearly drowned in the sea as he was walking on the water. John the Baptist, whom Jesus called the greatest born of woman, wondered while in prison whether Jesus was indeed the Christ, asking if he should look to another. So we are not alone. We find ourselves in this very human broken and dysfunctional family, which also happens to be God's family. We are no different than they: We struggle with times of doubt, we lack faith, and we begin to slip away, falling every so quickly.

These men and women of the Bible are given to us as examples. They might have lived a long time ago with their own problems and pains, their warts and wrinkles, faults and foibles, but their struggle with faith is universal. Faith means that we put our trust in something. I may put my faith in my job, thinking that my job will provide for me and save me from trouble. But we all know that this is not good news. Our jobs often fail us, as do our friends, family, and country. Even our spiritual leaders, our bishops and priests, can fail us too. As the psalmist reminds us, "Put not your trust in princes, in a son of man, in whom there is no help" (Ps 146:3). While other people may fail us, God will never fail us. His Word always comes to us as a Word of hope and encouragement, a Word of faith leading us on the narrow way.

The one biblical character that I return to throughout the year is Job. Job confounds me. The story begins with Job and his seven sons and three fair daughters with his "seven thousand sheep, three thousand camels, five hundred yoke of oxen," and so forth. He has a loving wife and a great house. Everything is going well for Job. Then Satan approaches God and challenges him that if he has some time with any of God's creatures and tempts them enough, they will falter and reject God. In other words, Satan wants to prove how weak God's creatures really are. God tells him that he can do anything to the person except take his life. God even invites Satan to try out his experiment on Job. Well, the Book of Job is rather long. The short version goes like this:

Job's sons are killed in wars, his daughters are stolen, his lands are seized, and his wife leaves him. Not only that, but then Job is inflicted with bodily sores. He winds up sitting in ashes and wearing sackcloth, which is the biblical way of being in a state of mourning. Anyway, three of his so-called friends come to visit him. I say so-called because they really aren't friends. Each one comes and tells Job how dumb he is because he is suffering greatly. Well, after these men deliver their three speeches, Job never falters. At the end, after everything has been taken away from him — his wife, children, house, lands, and animals — he still has his faith in God. Job might not understand why this has happened to him, but he remains firm in his faith.

Job's story isn't so much about why there is suffering or why bad things happen to good people. It is a story of faith. I often offer this story to parishioners who are going through great tragedies. People need to be reassured about putting their faith and trust in God. When their lives seems to be falling apart, if their husband or wife or loved ones die, or they lose a job or home, they need to be reminded that at the end of the day they are left only with God. This brings me great comfort. Faith is not always easy. I often have my own doubts about what God is doing or not doing, but at the end there is only faith.

This battle between faith and doubt will always be there. It is the cross in our life that we have to carry. Always remember that even in times of doubt, in times of questioning and pondering, we should strive to maintain our faith!

Food for Thought

1. Can you recall a recent time when you had strong faith in God? What was the particular circumstance and what was the outcome of this situation?

2. Have you had a period in your life when you felt that God abandoned you or that you doubted his strength and power? How did this make you feel?

3. If you had times of doubt or darkness, you are not alone. Some of the greatest Christian leaders had extended periods of doubt and even despair, what St. John of the Cross called the "dark night of the soul." Mother Teresa's recently published journals reveal that, even though she was a great humanitarian, she had long periods of doubt when she thought that God abandoned her. Martin Luther King Jr, Thomas Merton, and others had similar feel-

ings. Don't give up—keep trusting in the Lord each and every day.

4. For further reading: Psalm 22:1–2, Matthew 8:10; Acts 3:16; 2 Corinthians 5:7

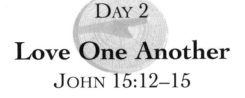

DAY 2

Love One Another
JOHN 15:12–15

"This is my commandment, that you love one another as I have loved you. No one has greater love than this, to lay down one's life for one's friends. You are my friends if you do what I command you. I do not call you servants any longer, because the servant does not know what the master is doing; but I have called you friends, because I have made known to you everything that I have heard from my Father."

There is no such thing as a perfect family. Do not let anyone fool you either! You may think that your family is perfect, but I guarantee you, that if you scratch the surface and look at your family in truthfulness and honesty you will notice all types of strange characters.

Everyone has an Uncle Johnny, who for some reason always tells inappropriate jokes in front of the children. No matter what you tell Uncle Johnny, he still doesn't understand that dirty jokes are not appropriate for five-year-olds. Or your Aunt Sue—you know, the one who always comes fashionably late for family events. If you tell her to come at 6 p.m. for dinner, she arrives at 6:30 p.m. or 6:45 p.m. If you invite her over for lunch at 12:30 p.m., she arrives at 1 p.m. or 1:15 p.m. You can tell Aunt Sue to come on time but she is always late. Then there is Aunt Margaret, who always has a dire need to complain about her perpetual ailments. Her bunions, backaches, and bursitis always seem to flare up during Thanksgiving dinner. And on and on we go, all types of colorful characters in our families, so many one often wonders if there is any hope to have a normal family.

Sometimes family members can do more than irritate us; often they can hurt us very badly. Whether it's a snide remark about our spouses or children, or maybe a rude comment about our body weight or hair color, words can be very powerful. Families often inflict cruel and unusual punishment on one another, even for no reason. Many people carry these feelings around with them for years, pushing these thoughts deep down into the inner chamber of their heart, where they fester and rot, making them angry and perhaps resentful at their mothers or fathers, brothers or sisters. Sometimes we might want to run away from our families. Some people actually do, never to return. The more time we spend with our families, the more time we rub against them and they rub against us, creating deep wounds. Sometimes our family members simply wear us down.

There are many examples given to us in the Bible about families in pain. Cain killed his brother Abel. Joseph's brothers beat him up, put him in a ditch, and left him for dead. James and John, the sons of Zebedee, always seemed to be arguing with Jesus about their future ministry and their place in the kingdom. Judas betrayed his own teacher and master.

The psalms tell us that the sins of the father are visited upon the seventh generation! I never knew my great-great-great-grandfather, but his problems and pain have somehow been incorporated into my life. The way he treated his wife and the way that he treated his sons and daughters are a part of my psychological makeup and DNA. It's a scary thought. The cycle continues and continues and continues. The pain and suffering are passed down to children and grandchildren. No wonder families are the way that they are these days!

Jesus entered into a human family not very different from our own. His parents, Mary and Joseph, raised him in a small village, Nazareth. We know from the scriptures that Jesus' cousins were Elizabeth, Zachariah, and John the Baptist. According to Church tradition, Jesus also had grandparents named Joachim and Anna. They were the parents of Mary and, like Abraham and Sarah in the Old Testament, they were too old to have children. However, after they had prayed and fasted for a long period, the Lord answered their prayer and gave them Mary. They agreed that she would be dedicated to God.

Jesus also had his close circle of disciples, who were very much a part of his extended family. These were a motley crew, to say the least! Some like Andrew and Peter were fishermen. Others like Matthew were tax collectors. They never seemed to get along. James and John were always bickering. Peter and Thomas seemed never to believe Jesus. Several times Jesus refers to these seemingly strong men as having little faith. One wonders if they even knew what Jesus was doing during this three-year ministry! Even Jesus' fatherly caregiver Joseph wanted to abandon the family because he didn't want to bear the shame of Mary being pregnant and they weren't even married yet. Thankfully, Joseph changed his mind.

The gospels portray Jesus' friends and family as far from perfect. From the very beginning of his life, we see this foreshadowed in his genealogy, which has come down to us through the Gospel of Matthew. A dark cast of characters is in Jesus' family lineage. Matthew doesn't specifically mention her by name, but "the wife of Uriah" is Bathsheba, whom David fell in love with. David had his loyal warrior Uriah sent into battle, knowing that Uriah would probably be killed and then he could marry Bathsheba. Their treacherous union brought forth Solomon, the great king who eventually built the Temple in Jerusalem. Then there is Rahab, the harlot who helped Joshua's spies survey the land, which allowed the Israelites to enter the Promised Land. Jesus' family is peppered with great and not-so-great people and personalities. Perhaps Matthew is showing us that the human condition is not so perfect after all, and God that entered this imperfect condition in order to restore it and bring healing to the world.

In other words, Jesus had a human family just like our family, but they were far from normal. His friends seemed to be no better either! They argued and doubted, and were very stubborn at times. They never seemed to understand his parables and teachings. But God doesn't leave us to our own devices; he brings his healing power to help restore our families to what they should be. He doesn't do it alone; he invites us to help him. We have an active part to play in healing the pain and suffering in our families.

You might think that I painted a terrible portrait of the family. However, we also know from the Bible that healing can take place. Love covers up a multitude of sins. The more we love others as Jesus loves us, the more our sins are wiped away. So if we regularly show love, then our families will hopefully seek healing. As Jesus said, "Love one another as I have loved you." Love is not easy. I often have a very difficult time loving people who drive me crazy or who don't always agree with my ideas about religion, politics, or culture. I even find that sometimes the ones we love the most are the ones who drive us the craziest! I guess this is what it means to be human.

Before Jesus left his disciples, he told them that they were supposed to go out into the world and preach and teach forgiveness of sins, and that repentance be proclaimed in his name. So forgiveness also has a big part to play in the healing process. Forgiveness is not just saying, "I am sorry," but actually involves a complete and total confession of guilt and remorse. Forgiveness requires that we make amends for the wrongs that we have done in life. According to Jesus, forgiveness is not optional, it is a major condition for the spiritual life. "If you do not forgive the sins of your brother, neither will God the father forgive you." Those are strong words from Jesus. Forgiveness is not easy but it is a great way to bring healing to one's family, especially for those who tend to rub us the wrong way.

God provides us with many opportunities for wholeness and holiness. We certainly cannot choose the members of our family, but we can choose whether we will pass our anger, resentment, and bad feelings onto our children, grandchildren, and even great-grandchildren. Or, we can choose to practice love, truthfulness, and forgiveness, passing God's love on to those who come after us. Not only will we pass this wonderful gift onto our grandchildren, but also perhaps we can help heal the pain, suffering, and dysfunction of our parents and grandparents. What a wonderful gift we have been given in the name of Jesus!

Food for Thought

1. Do you have relatives in your family like an "Uncle Johnny" or "Aunt Sue" who are difficult people? How do you react toward them?

2. We can become more gentle and loving if we do not focus so much on people's faults, foibles, warts, and wrinkles, but on the good and positive aspects of their personality. This week try to focus on the good qualities in the people around you, your friends, coworkers, and extended family.

3. For further reading: John 3:16; 1 Corinthians 13; 1 John 4:7–12

Day 3

Peace Be with You
John 20:19–23

When it was evening on that day, the first day of the week, and the doors of the house where the disciples had met were locked for fear of the Jews, Jesus came and stood among them and said, "Peace be with you." After he said this, he showed them his hands and his side. Then the disciples rejoiced when they saw the Lord. Jesus said to them again, "Peace be with you. As the Father has sent me, so I send you." When he had said this, he breathed on them and said to them, "Receive the Holy Spirit. If you forgive the sins of any, they are forgiven them; if you retain the sins of any, they are retained."

Every year, in the little town of Bethlehem, Christians from across the world gather together to offer their praise and prayer in celebration of Jesus' birth. They come together with anticipation and joy as they walk in the footsteps of Joseph, Mary, the shepherds, and wise men. They make a pilgrimage to the birthplace of the Son of God. The Church of the Nativity in Manger Square is a living witness to the birth of Jesus. People flock to see where it has been said that Jesus was born. They make their way through a dark cavern in the basement of the Church of the Nativity. When they walk through a small doorway, they see a silver star in a little niche carved out of the wall where people say that Jesus was born. They light candles, offering prayers and worshipping God.

They leave with a sense of hope that their prayers will be heard and answered. Like us, they share the joy of this wonderful event.

Despite the hope that the pilgrims bring, the citizens of Bethlehem have to endure many hardships because of a large thirty-foot-tall wall that surrounds much of the city, separating families, friends, and neighbors from one another. Bethlehem is currently in the West Bank, which has been walled off from the rest of Israel; families and friends have been separated by this wall. The citizens of Bethlehem have a hard time traveling even to nearby Jerusalem for shopping. Finding work is even more difficult, given the fact that there are few jobs around.

This is daily life in Bethlehem. Not much has changed in two thousand years. Two thousand years ago, in the very same town of Bethlehem, the wise men came seeking the newborn King and told Herod where he was to be born. Herod, of course, was afraid of this baby; he was paranoid that *his* kingship would be short lived. The wise men from the East made a long journey across the desert in order to pay homage and to offer their worship to the newborn child in the village of Bethlehem. But they, like the Christians in Palestine, were stopped along the way.

Then, as today, Bethlehem was a very small place, never large like Jerusalem, Antioch, or Rome. But Bethlehem was where King David was born, too. He was the only king in Israel who could unite the twelve tribes, who were constantly bickering, fighting, and arguing, and who seemed always to be at each other's throats. These tribes acted like brothers constantly fighting. Despite the fact that the tribes couldn't get along, David came along one day bringing peace, uniting them into one nation.

Bethlehem was the birthplace of David, one of the great Old Testament kings, and the place where the prophet Samuel anointed David to be the king (1 Sam 16:4). Likewise, Ephratha was the burial place of Rachel, the wife of Jacob. "So Rachel died, and she was buried on the way to Ephratha (that is Bethlehem), and Jacob set up a pillar upon her grave; it is the pillar of Rachel's tomb, which is there to this day. Israel journeyed on, and pitched his tent beyond the tower of Eder" (Gen 35:19). It is here in this small part of the world, in a faraway place called Bethlehem, where God chose to take flesh and make his home among us.

Centuries later, in this very same town, one greater than David was about to be born, Christ the Lord, the Prince of Peace, whom we honor and worship at Christmas. Jesus brings us the peace of God, the eternal peace, what the Hebrews called the *shalom* of God. This *shalom* is not from men, not from governments, not from committees, but from God. The angels announced, "Glory to God in the highest heaven, and on earth peace among those whom he favors!" (Luke 2:14).

A similar statement of peace is attributed to Jesus in the Gospel of John. After his resurrection he comes to his disciples in the Upper Room in Jerusalem where they had their last Passover meal together, and he says, "Peace be with you. As the Father has sent me, even so I send you." This is the *shalom* from God himself.

During our life we find ourselves in the middle of wars and arguments, encountering walls not too much different from that around Bethlehem. We are in a war in Iraq, in Afghanistan; civil wars are always erupting in countries throughout the world. Our country constantly seems to be in a war on poverty, drugs, sexism, racism; in a war against abuse and violence; and probably the most important war, the war that divides each of our hearts. This war is the most damaging because it is ongoing. From the first breath of our life to the very last one, we are fighting a battle of faith versus doubt, light versus darkness, truth versus falsehood, and good versus evil. This battle is constant. Jesus comes to us in his gospel, coming as our peace, our *shalom*, our new David; coming not only to help us, but to fight for us in our daily struggles with darkness, doubt, and despair. Jesus is Immanuel, whose name literally means *God with us*. He comes to us and fights for us against the evil in this world, as we pray in the Lord's Prayer, "and deliver us from evil." Jesus comes to unite our hearts, to make us whole again, bringing the peace of God into our life.

Some human beings did not yearn for peace: Lenin. Hitler. Stalin. Mussolini. Idi Amin. Mao Zedong. One by one, individuals gather supporters who rally in their cause to fight. One by one, these forces of evil gather together, gaining momentum, and begin to wage war — war between countries, races, nations, and peoples. They get swept up in the moment; in an emotional uproar, they fire guns and drop bombs. They lead massacres and holocausts. They conquer and kill.

Thankfully, to counteract the forces of evil, there are the peacekeepers, people who have always sought peace and serenity among humanity: Jesus. Paul. Gandhi.

Martin Luther King, Jr. Daniel Berrigan. Dorothy Day. Edith Stein. Dietrich Bonhoeffer. Individuals stand up to war; they stand against social injustice, poverty, sexism, and racism. Individuals can be ambassadors of peace in this world, making it a better place for you and for me.

All Christians are called to be ambassadors of peace. We cannot wait for someone else to do it. Jesus' birth in that faraway village of Bethlehem reminds us of our common calling to bring God's *shalom* to the world so that it will be a better place for everyone. If each of us can make our little corner of the world a little more peaceful, then each and every corner will be a little better. We can leave this world in a little better shape than how we found it.

Food for Thought

1. Take a few moments and think about the wars and battles that are raging in the world today. About the wars and battles in your family or at work or in school.

2. Take a few moments and think of someone in your life who you look to as a peacekeeper. How do they maintain peace and concord in their life?

3. Are you striving to be an ambassador of peace? Is it easy or difficult? How can you become a better peacemaker and make the world a better place?

4. For further reading: Psalm 34:11–14; John
   20:19–23; 2 Corinthians 13:14

DAY 4

Whose Child Is This?
LUKE 2:21–32

*After eight days had passed, it was time to circumcise the child;
and he was called Jesus, the name given by the angel before he
was conceived in the womb. And when the time came for their
purification according to the law of Moses, they brought him
up to Jerusalem to present him to the Lord (as it is written in
the law of the Lord, "Every male that opens the womb shall be
called holy to the Lord"), and they offered a sacrifice according
to what is said in the law of the Lord, "a pair of turtledoves, or
two young pigeons."*

In ancient Judaism it was customary to name a child
eight days after birth. The idea was that when a child was
given a name, this name was written in the Book of Life,
and when the messiah returned at the Last Judgment he
would know all of the names of the people who lived from
the beginning of the world to the end of the world. He
would know the names of every single person in the
entire universe. Today some Christian groups still maintain this very ancient practice of naming a child on the
eighth day of its birth as a testimony to God's commandment. Conversely, to have one's name blotted out or

destroyed was as if the person no longer existed: "Their roots dry up beneath, and their branches wither above. Their memory perishes from the earth and they have no name in the street" (Job 18:17). This is why in the Old Testament there was a strict taboo against profaning the name of the Lord, because in doing so they were profaning the Lord himself: "You shall not make wrongful use of the name of the LORD God, for the LORD will not acquit anyone who misuses his name" (Exod 20:7). To have one's name changed is to have one's identity changed as well.

There are numerous scriptural examples of name changes. In Genesis 17, God told his servant Abram that he would be the father of many nations and promised to make his covenant with him.

> *"I am God Almighty, walk before me, and be blameless. And I will make my covenant between me and you, and will multiply you exceedingly." Then Abram fell on his face; and God said to him, "Behold, my covenant is with you, and you shall be the father of a multitude of nations. No longer shall your name be Abram, but your name shall be Abraham; for I have made you the father of a multitude of nations."* (Gen 17:1–6)

Likewise, Abraham's wife had her name changed from Sarai to Sarah after she found out that in her old age she would bear the child Isaac. Jacob's name was changed to Israel after he wrestled with the angel of the Lord (Gen 32:28). In the New Testament, Saul the Pharisee, who persecuted Christians and assisted with the stoning of Stephen, had his name changed from Saul to Paul (Acts 13:9).

We know from the Gospel of Luke that Mary and Joseph fulfilled the angel's command and called the baby Jesus, which is the Greek form of the Hebrew name for Joshua, which means *savior*. Joshua the son of Nun was a famous leader in the Old Testament. He was a friend of Moses and was a leader of the Israelite people. Just before he died, Moses named Joshua to be his successor. Joshua led the Israelites into Canaan, the land of milk and honey. According to the Israelites, Joshua was very much their savior, saving them from the hand of the Egyptians.

Naming a child is very practical. After all, if you have three, four, or five children, it is much easier to give them a name to differentiate between them than if they had no name. If we didn't have a name we would just call each other boy, girl, man, or woman; or child A, B, or C. That would be very strange. I cannot imagine naming a child daughter B or son A. A name designates our individuality as persons. Even as early as the Book of Genesis, we know that when God finished his creation and made Adam, God invited Adam to name the animals in creation, differentiating one from another.

In addition to our given name at birth, we are also given other names as well. Very often our teachers, friends, parents, and relatives give us names such as wonderful, nice, cute, beautiful, intelligent, and funny. These are nice names to have. However, sometimes people call us unflattering names, names that make us feel bad inside. Names like ugly, stupid, dumb, naughty, and no good. We might feel inadequate or awkward when we hear these names. We might feel embarrassed and upset. Psychologists tell us that, if someone calls us a particular name long enough, we begin to believe in that name. In other words, if we are in kindergarten and someone calls us a dummy all the time, we might begin to think that we are indeed dumb, even though we might be intelligent and smart. If other children call us dummy, then our negative feelings will be reinforced, and we will think that we are *really* dumb. We can actually become our name.

Names are like labels; they stick to us. These names get piled on, one after another. The names that are given to us in our earliest years are the ones that stick the most. We never forget them. When I was in first grade some of my classmates called me, "Billy the Jolly Green Giant," after the popular television advertisement for frozen vegetables. I was very tall for my age and I really stuck out among my classmates. I hated that name. Every time I heard it I wanted to cry. This name really hurt my feelings. Other children in school are called harsh names like fat, stupid, and dumb. Looking back, I pity those other children. They must have felt just as bad as I did.

In Japan, there is an ancient form of theater called Kabuki, which is performed to this day. All of the actors are men, but they use different masks so they can play both male and female parts. These masks replace makeup. There are masks for characters that are sad, happy, excited, or mad. It is only at the end of the play when the actors remove the masks that we see their true identity. During the course of a play, an actor will wear many masks. How many masks do we wear in life? How many different labels do we have? When does the real me and the real you come through? Are we merely actors on this stage of life, walking and acting out our names that are given to us? Are we just the sum total of our masks that we wear?

It is time to start ripping off these labels one by one, yanking them off and throwing them away. We need to get rid of these fake masks that we wear day in and day out. We are living a lie if we don't. We will never allow the real me, and the real you, the person that God wants us to be, come through. God doesn't want us to live fake and false lives. He wants us to be authentic human beings just like he created us to be. He wants us to be real, true to ourselves, and true to the world around us.

The only person in the world who was the most real and truly authentic was Jesus. From the very beginning of his life, he knew who he was and what God wanted from him. He didn't wear masks, even though people certainly called him a host of names: "Is this Jesus, the son of Joseph, the carpenter's son?" or "He casts out demons by the prince of demons." Jesus' own name is very powerful weapon against the evil in this world. The Book of Acts tells us that the apostles used his name to cure the sick, raise the dead, and drive out demons. We even pray through his name, "We ask this of you O Lord in Jesus' name. Amen." The power of the name is great and we are to cherish and use this name forever.

Food for Thought

1. School aged children are often not very nice to one another and call each other bad names. Think back to your childhood. Were you called

names in school? How did these names make you feel?

2. The scriptures tell us that love and forgiveness cover up a multitude of sins and are the ingredients to wholeness and holiness. If you hold any anger or resentment against other people, especially for things done to you a long time ago, let it go. Life is too short to be angry and hold grudges.

3. For further reading: Micah 4:5; Mark 9:38–41; Acts 4:10–12; Colossians 3:17

DAY 5

Let Your Light Shine
MATTHEW 5:14–16

"You are the light of the world. A city built on a hill cannot be hidden. No one after lighting a lamp puts it under the bushel basket, but on the lampstand, and it gives light to all in the house. In the same way, let your light shine before others, so that they may see your good works and give glory to your Father in heaven."

Every so often we encounter a major scandal in our government, Church, or local municipality: Watergate, Enron, the Iran Contra affair, and all types of sexual misconduct and abuse of minors. The list goes on and on. Almost every week a new scandal erupts somewhere around the country. Some of these are like a soap opera; they last for weeks on end. Most of these scandals begin as deep dark secrets that get hidden deep away in someone's life or the life of a company or a group of people. Once the news gets out, there is no stopping it.

How many of us have our own little dirty secrets, our own family scandals and dark mysteries that we keep hidden in the deepest closets of our hearts? Tales of pain and suffering, the hidden hurts of childhood, are kept in our hearts, like old laundry. And it gets worse. Every time we have a secret or a little family scandal, we keep adding it to the pile that is already there, the pile gets bigger and bigger, and like laundry, it stinks to high heaven. So often these family secrets, these scandals that never see the light of day, destroy us from the inside out. They eat us alive, destroying our humanity. We become cold and callous, angry bitter people who have a hard time loving others.

One of the gospel stories that I return to again and again is the story of the Samaritan woman. Here is this woman who is coming to Jacob's well to draw water. She is a Samaritan. Jews did not socialize with the Samaritans. Actually they hated the Samaritans. The Jews considered them half-breeds because they were partly Jewish and partly pagan. They had mixed religious beliefs and customs. The Samaritans were considered outcasts and hence were unclean. Just the fact that Jesus, who was basically like a Jewish rabbi, would talk to this Samaritan woman was alone countercultural. Anyway, through the course of their conversation, we learn that this woman not only had one husband but had five husbands, and Jesus tells her that even the man that she is living with currently is not her husband! However, even though Jesus could have condemned her and even have her stoned, he chose another route. He never accuses her of wrongdoing or makes her feel guilty. He treats her like any human person with love and respect. She runs and tells her fellow Samaritans all that he has done for her. We can learn a lot from this brief interaction. Jesus merely cast some light of the truth on the situation, and she literally became an apostle to her own people, and as John says, "Many Samaritans from that city believed in him because of the woman's testimony" (John 4:39). Jesus brought her the light of truth. She literally saw the light and believed.

Matthew reminds us that Jesus is the light that shines in the darkness. Jesus appears to the world for the first time as a beacon of light shining brightly in the world, like a lighthouse shining across the seashore. However, we too are lights. Jesus tells his disciples that they are supposed to let their light shine so that other people can see. If we let our light shine brightly, then others can see the works of being done in Jesus' name and that they too may see and believe. We shouldn't try to hide this light but to share it with others. The Gospel of John has a similar expression about Jesus' ministry. At the miracle of the healing of the man born blind, Jesus says, "I am the light of the world." Then he heals the man by taking some of his own spit and mixing it with mud from the ground, and then tells the man to go wash in a pool of water. The man returns with his sight intact.

When we read the gospels, we realize that the light of Christ exposes all of our deep dark secrets so that we can see them for what they truly are. We can name our demons and sins and then let them go. We cannot see our own sin if we do not have light. Jesus enters into our pain and suffering and brokenness and brings healing. A few hundred years before Jesus, the prophet Isaiah put it this way: "Arise, shine; for your light has come, and the glory of the Lord has risen upon you. For darkness shall cover the earth, and thick darkness the peoples; but the Lord will arise upon you, and his glory will appear over you. Nations shall come to your light, and kings to the brightness of your dawn" (Isa 60:1–3).

Food for Thought

1. Take some time and make a list of the persons whom you have offended or who have offended you. Pray for these people. The power of prayer is truly awesome. Offer their names up in prayer and place your burdens on God. He will do the rest.

2. The sacrament of confession, or reconciliation, is a powerful spiritual practice that helps us deal with our family secrets, scandals, and pain. It is comforting to confess one's sins to a priest and be able to get some spiritual insight and direction afterward. If you do not have a relationship with a priest, you might want to visit with a spiritual director. Spiritual directors are fellow persons of faith who will help

guide and lead you to a deeper understanding of the work of the Holy Spirit in your life.

3. For further reading: Psalm 27; Isaiah 2:5–11; John 1:4–9; Romans 13:12

DAY 6

Do You See What I See?
LUKE 18:35–39

As he approached Jericho, a blind man was sitting by the road-side begging. When he heard a crowd going by, he asked what was happening. They told him, "Jesus of Nazareth is passing by." Then he shouted, "Jesus, Son of David, have mercy on me!" Those who were in front sternly ordered him to be quiet; but he shouted even more loudly, "Son of David, have mercy on me!"

So much of our life is perception. One time I had the opportunity to visit forty elementary school children at a local Lutheran parochial school. Once in a while pastors from the local community call me to present some aspect of the Eastern Orthodox faith to schoolchildren or college students. After spending some time thinking about what to say to these youngsters, I decided to speak about icons. Children love "show and tell," so I decided to bring our icon of the Virgin Mary with the baby Jesus. I wanted to talk about Mary's role as Jesus' mother and how she is the mother of all Christians. This icon shows

Mary in the middle of the picture wearing a blue and maroon tunic and holding the baby Jesus off to one side. Her face is golden brown with hints of amber and around her head is a gold circle, what we call a halo.

At the end of my brief presentation I asked if the children had questions. Of course I was a bit scared—you never know what a second grader might ask! A young boy asked why there was a sun around Mary's head! His question caught me off guard. A sun? I looked at the icon and noticed that, where *I* saw a golden halo around her head, *he* saw a golden sun. After studying the icon for a moment, I concluded that indeed her halo looked like a sun. I then explained to him that this was a halo and in our faith tradition a halo signifies that the person in the picture is very special, what we call a saint, or a holy person. Something very ordinary and common to me wasn't ordinary and common to everyone. There was a difference in perception.

The question about Mary's halo made me think about perception. So much of our life depends on how we perceive things. I can take a mug and fill it halfway with coffee. Someone looking at the cup might see it as half full, others will see it as half empty. If I witness a car accident, I may think that the blue car crossed over the line and hit the red car. Another witness may say that the red car crossed over the line and hit the blue car. Again, a case of perception, or even misperception, of what actually took place.

Many people in the gospels had the wrong perception of Jesus' identity. When people in the villages saw Jesus pass by, they saw Jesus the teacher. Or others may have seen Jesus the miracle worker. Others saw Jesus the son of Joseph, the carpenter's son. Still others saw Jesus the king or the prophet. However, these perceptions wee limited and narrow. Jesus was from Nazareth and *was* the son of a carpenter, but he was more than that. He *was* a teacher, but he did more than just teach. He *was* a prophet but he was more than a prophet.

The blind man Bartimaeus perceived something greater about Jesus, that he was the Son of David. This short title describes Jesus to a T. The Son of David refers to the Messiah, and as the Messiah he is also our savior. Ironically, Bartimaeus was blind. He couldn't see two feet in front of him, yet the people in the crowds and who were standing along the way really didn't know who Jesus was. The questions put to us today are: Who do we think Jesus is? Is he the son of Joseph, the carpenter's son? Is Jesus the miracle worker, who performs miracles that razzle and dazzle us? Is Jesus the great teacher who teaches us about living the good life? Is he a miracle worker, a spiritual guru who comes to heal us from our sickness? Or is he more than that?

Very often we create our own picture of Jesus. They are really false idols, fake and phony, just like the golden calf at the bottom of Mount Sinai. It is very comfortable to have a controllable Jesus in our minds. People tend to focus on the Jesus that we want to believe in: the teacher, the simple carpenter of Nazareth, the miracle worker, or the judge. Yet Jesus is the sum total of these. He is the very son of God. We cannot pick and choose who we want Jesus to be. We need to focus on Jesus as he is!

The Bible destroys our false images and idols of Jesus. When reading the Bible we begin to search and seek for Jesus in the scriptures. Our images begin to fade away, the idols are destroyed, and the real Jesus, the Jesus of the gospels, the Jesus of the scriptures—Jesus, the Son of God, the Son of David—is formed in our heads and in our hearts so that we can worship the one true living Jesus, the one who comes and feeds us each and every day. Our false images and idols are deleted from our mental hard drive, erased, and the true Jesus, the one whom Paul proclaimed, is formed once again in our hearts and minds.

Food for Thought

1. When thinking about Jesus, people often had a very narrow view of his ministry. Some saw him as merely a teacher, a miracle worker, or a prophet. When thinking about Jesus, what comes to your mind? Does anything in particular stick out in regards to Jesus' life and ministry?

2. Jesus was a social and cultural rebel, going against the common religious and cultural assumptions of his day. In other words, Jesus was countercultural. How can we express this countercultural activity in our daily life? How can we be faithful to Jesus and the gospel and yet at the same time be countercultural?

3. For further reading: Psalm 115:1–8; Ezekiel
    12:1–6; Matthew 8:23–27; Luke 4:20–22

DAY 7

Today Salvation Has Come
LUKE 19:1–10

*He entered Jericho and was passing through it. A man was
there named Zacchaeus; he was a chief tax collector and was
rich. He was trying to see who Jesus was, but on account of the
crowd he could not, because he was short in stature. So he ran
ahead and climbed a sycamore tree to see him, because he was
going to pass that way.*

When Jesus entered Jericho, he encountered a man
named Zacchaeus. Luke tells us that he was no ordinary
man but a chief tax collector who was very rich. We also
know that Levi was a tax collector but as soon as he met
Jesus, he left his tax booth and followed him. His name
was later changed from Levi to Matthew and he became
one of Jesus' disciples. Tradition says that he authored
the Gospel of Matthew. These are the only two passages
where we are told that Jesus encountered a chief tax
collector.

In the ancient world, the Roman government levied
various types of taxes on the people in the empire in order
to generate revenue. Many of these tax collectors served
as subcontractors. They would collect the tax for the

Romans, but they would also include a high commission in order to bolster their meager salary. We are not told directly about Zacchaeus' pedigree but since he has a Jewish name, it is most likely that he was a Jew. Thus, Zacchaeus was a Jew working for the Roman Empire, which to the eyes of many Jewish people was an outrage. We need to keep in mind that the Roman Empire was in full control over the entire area, and Zacchaeus was probably seen as a traitor or at least collaborating with the enemy, very similar to the Vichy government in France during World War II that collaborated with the Nazi government.

Zacchaeus wanted to see Jesus, but got more than he bargained for because Jesus told him that he wanted to come to his house. This was more than a dinner invitation. To be invited to someone's house meant that they wanted to share fellowship with that person. In other words Jesus overlooked the fact that he was a tax collector and wanted to go visit with him. Jesus' comment instilled anger in the crowd as they said, "He has gone to be the guest of one who is a sinner" (Luke 19:7).

We were not given details to exactly why he climbed up that tree; he heard that Jesus was passing by that way. We don't know if Zacchaeus had heard about Jesus before, but only that he must have had a deep desire to see Jesus. Jesus called him down saying, "Zacchaeus, hurry and come down; for I must stay at your house today." Come down now. Jesus called Zacchaeus down from that tree because he wanted to visit Zacchaeus's house. Jesus offered him a new lease on life, a second chance for Zacchaeus. No longer would he cheat people on their taxes or take a little *extra gravy* from the top like many executives do at companies these days. No, Jesus brought new life to Zacchaeus and his family. Zacchaeus heard that call to new life and responded. He didn't stay up there in that tree. He didn't say to himself, "Well, Jesus will come again sometime in the future." No, he climbed down and welcomed Jesus into his home. All this waiting was over, the Messiah had arrived!

Imagine that your best friend promised to send you a package through the United Parcel Service (UPS). Every day you look out your window for that UPS truck as it comes down your street, but it doesn't stop at your house. It passes right by. So the next day you go and look outside your window and wait for that UPS truck and he doesn't stop, he drives right by. And the third day you wait for that UPS truck and it drives right by. After a few days you will get tired of waiting for that UPS truck. However, this is what Zacchaeus was doing, he was waiting for God's salvation to arrive—and it finally did arrive!

Salvation has come, it is here! Jesus has come to our house! Every time we gather we are responding to God's call to faith. We are hearing God speak to us. May we always have the eyes to see and the ears to hear God speaking and to respond to this call in faith and in love, always seeking to follow him all the days of our life!

Food for Thought

1. If Jesus said that he was coming to your house for dinner tonight, how would you respond to this invitation? Would your family be pre-

pared to host Jesus? Would you decline his invitation or would you accept it?

2. One theme in this gospel story is attentive listening. Jesus told Zacchaeus that he was coming to his house for dinner. Zacchaeus listened to Jesus' words and followed them. How can we better listen to Jesus today? How can we open our lives to him each and every day?

3. For further reading: Psalm 62:1–7; Habakkuk 3:13–18; Philippians 2:12–13

DAY 8

The Man in the Mirror
LUKE 18:10–14

He also told this parable to some who trusted in themselves that they were righteous and regarded others with contempt: "Two men went up to the temple to pray, one a Pharisee and the other a tax-collector. The Pharisee, standing by himself, was praying thus, 'God, I thank you that I am not like other people: thieves, rogues, adulterers, or even like this tax collector. I fast twice a week; I give a tenth of all my income.' But the tax collector, standing far off, would not even look up to heaven, but was beating his breast and saying, 'God, be merciful to me, a sinner!' I tell you, this man went down to his home justified rather than the other; for all who exalt themselves will be humbled, but all who humble themselves will be exalted."

Did you commit a murder this week? What about a bank robbery? Maybe you bribed a coworker or tried to blackmail someone? If you are reading this book, I am sure that you didn't do any of these things! These crimes are considered the *biggies* and very few people commit heinous crimes. If you stand in the middle of downtown in an American city, surveying people passing by, you will most likely get the same answer. The average person does not commit major crimes like murder, bank robbery, or bribery. Perhaps the most you will find are a few unpaid traffic tickets or a minor offense such as petty theft.

However, were you jealous this week? Were you unkind and unloving toward your spouse and children? Did you get angry and lash out at someone at work? Most of us are guilty of these somewhat small offences. While most people do not commit big sins, we do commit the small, petty ones like jealousy, anger, or being unkind. We might not think that these small offences are that important; after all, how can you compare stealing a car with being unkind to someone?

However, we shouldn't feel so smug. These small, seemingly innocuous sins add up! According to the Bible, a sin is a sin is a sin. In God's eyes, if we do not love him with all our hearts, souls, strength, and minds and our neighbor as ourselves, we are in big trouble. This is basically the sin of the Pharisee; his prayer to God was that he was not that bad because he did not commit murder, adultery, or extortion. He was just an average Pharisee praying in the Temple, telling God how good he was.

The Pharisee and the publican were not that different. On the one hand, we have a tax collector and the

Pharisee who are both in the Temple praying to God. The Pharisee offered a prayer that was basically a long list of his good qualities. His prayer included no contrition of heart for any suffering or pain that he inflicted on others.

Then we see the publican at prayer, and he prays in a radically different way. He stands at the back of the Temple, praying in a very sincere and open manner, and beating his breast, saying, "God, be merciful to me a sinner." He is very sorry for what he has done in his life and is asking God for mercy and compassion. Jesus ends this short parable with a simple phrase: "For all who exalt themselves will be humbled, but all who humble themselves will be exalted" (Luke 18:14).

The parable is about humility. The publican prayed in a humble way, simply acknowledging his sinfulness without making excuses or rationalizing the bad things that he has done, not heaping up long prayers but in a contrite and simple manner: God be merciful to me, a sinner. The publican offered the more acceptable prayer than did the Pharisee and, as Jesus says, was justified.

The gospels show us that Jesus came preaching a gospel of humility. His preaching stirred up the traditional cultural, religious, and social norms of his day. He spent time with harlots, publicans, Samaritans, lepers, as well as adulterers and Gentiles. He ate with prostitutes and tax collectors and spent most of his time with the outcasts of society. Jesus reached out to people on the margins of society and welcomed them to God's house, bringing his saving message to anyone who had ears to hear. Meanwhile the children of Abraham, God's chosen people, seemed to have hardened hearts and stiff necks and did not want to hear the good news. Yet Jesus kept on preaching this good news until his very last breath. It was for the sick that he came, not the healthy.

Food for Thought

1. The parable of the publican and the Pharisee shows two men at prayer. The Pharisee's prayer was self-centered, focusing on the good things that he had accomplished in life. On the other hand, we have the prayer of the publican, which was a prayer of humility: "God have mercy on me, a sinner." Can we pray this prayer along with the publican?

2. The word *sin* in Greek means to miss the mark, as if we were shooting an arrow into a bull's-eye and the arrow misses. It is considered off the mark and therefore a sin. Sins are not only things that we do wrong, such as lie, steal, or cheat, but also includes things that we should do but we don't, like being more loving, forgiving others, being more generous with our time, talents, and treasure. Take a few moments and make a list of your sins and things that you have done to offend someone else in your life. After looking at this list, how do you feel? Are there ways to make amends for your sins?

3. For further reading: Psalm 51; Isaiah 58; Mark 1:14–15

DAY 9

A Long and Wending Road
LUKE 15:11–24

Then Jesus said, "There was a man who had two sons. The younger of them said to his father, 'Father, give me the share of the property that will belong to me.' So he divided his property between them. And a few days later the younger son gathered all he had and traveled to a distant country, and there he squandered his property in dissolute living. And when he had spent everything, a great famine arose in that country, and he began to be in want. So he went and joined himself to one of the citizens of that country who sent him into his fields to feed swine. And he would gladly have fed on the pods that the swine ate; and no one gave him anything."

What is it about teenagers that drive parents crazy? Is it that they stay out late and don't call to let us know when they will be returning home? Or is it that they spend their money on frivolous things like junk food, clothes, and music? Or is it because teenagers think that they "know it all" and that their parents are dumb? Parents quickly forget that they too were teenagers once and probably gave their parents the same headaches and problems when they were young.

The context for the parable of the prodigal son is revealed in the opening verses of the chapter: "Now tax collectors and sinners were all drawing near to hear him. And the Pharisees and the scribes murmured, saying,

'This fellow welcomes sinners and eats with them'" (Luke 15:1–2). Throughout the Gospel of Luke we have seen how Jesus goes out of his way to those on the margins of society, the blind and the lame, the demon-possessed, those who are ritually impure, and the Gentile Roman soldiers. As we saw previously with the person of Zacchaeus, Jesus even offers his hand of hospitality to tax collectors and government workers. Jesus breaks all social and political mores and expectations in order to show that he is bringing a prophetic word that is the gospel of salvation. This gospel is one that changes and alters our common thinking and understanding.

Luke tells us that a man had two sons and one of these sons asked for his inheritance. This might seem like a normal request; however, we also have to remember that in antiquity the eldest son inherited everything. Yet already we see something different happening. The father concedes and gives the youngest son his portion. The youngest son leaves and goes off into a far country while the eldest son remains with the father.

The story continues with some important details. The youngest son squandered his possessions in loose living. He also found himself in hunger and want since a famine arose in that country. In order to survive, the young man had to live amongst outsiders, since Luke says that his job was feeding pigs. Jewish purity laws forbade them to deal with pork products and we can infer that these people were either Gentiles or non-law-abiding Jews. In any case he seemed to hit bottom. He left his father and home, lost all his possessions, was hungry, and had to feed the pigs.

However, the young boy wanted to return home and made up a speech that he was going to tell his father. Yet as he was returning to his father, the father ran out and welcomed his son home. The father didn't ask questions, did not accuse his son of wasting his time and money, and did not say "I told you so." Rather, the father immediately told his servants to prepare a celebration for his son. The story doesn't end there. All the while, the eldest son who never left the father was upset that the father was making such a big celebration for his other son. In other words, he was jealous that the father never gave him a party. The father responded to the son by saying, "Son, you are always with me, and all that is mine is yours. But we had to celebrate and rejoice, because the brother of yours was dead and has come to life; he was lost and has been found" (Luke 15:31–32), which is repeated earlier in Luke 15:24. Just as the father in this story forgave and welcomed back his son, so too does the Lord welcome us back as well.

I have always found this story to be very comforting: that no matter how far I seem to stray from the narrow path, following my own selfish desires, the Lord is always there running out to welcome me. This is a very humbling experience, knowing that no matter how far we go away, no matter what we do, we are welcomed back, with open arms, with God's never-ending mercy, compassion, and forgiveness which is seen in the prayer of confession.

This theme of reconciliation and forgiveness is expressed so beautifully in the sacrament of confession. When we go to confession, we go with a spirit of humility, confessing our sins to the priest. Like the younger son in the parable, we have wasted so much of our time, talents, and treasure on loose living, very often following our own hearts' desire rather than following the Lord. Not only do we come confessing our sins, but we also seek advice from our priest, who like us is also a sinner. Our priest will try to direct us back on the narrow way to the kingdom, focusing our attention on the one needful thing, which is being obedient to Christ. Hopefully we leave confession with a clean heart, seeking once again to serve both God and neighbor in our life. When we fall again, we will be welcomed back with open arms, once again, receiving the mercy, love, and compassion of God.

Throughout our journey we have heard of many miracles and teachings from Jesus. We know that Luke speaks of Jesus as the great savior of the world, the Lord's Messiah who brings the gospel to the whole world, to the Gentiles or nations. In many ways we are like the Gentiles, living in darkness and the shadow of death, yet once again the gospel is proclaimed to us, as it was the first time in Palestine a long time ago.

Luke does not give us precise details about the age of the young man, but in my mind he was very much like a teenager. Didn't he do the same things that most teenagers do? He took his money, slammed the door, and left home, entering a self-imposed exile, running away from both father and family to live his own life. He left the house never looking back. He also probably said, "I don't need my parents anymore, I can live on my own." How many parents have heard this line before?

Spending his money on loose living, or in our modern lingo *living large*, did not get the boy very far. His gas tank was quickly running on empty. He worked minimum-wage jobs just to survive. In our culture we would say that he would probably be working in a convenience store or cleaning floors, menial labor at best. But as most teens he came groveling back home. He even made up a sad story to tell his father. Well, of course his father knew best and left the light on, waiting for his son to return. Teens usually return home for a hot meal and a warm cozy bed. His son was no different; he came home on his hands and knees begging to return. But his father didn't let him give his speech. He ran out, greeted him, and gave him a big welcome-home party.

We might be adults, but a small teenager always exists way deep inside of us that never really left when we became an adult. Don't we still push God out of our life, wandering off into far and distant lands? Don't we waste our time and energy following dreams and ideas that don't pile up to anything productive and wholesome, and often just fulfill our vanity and pride? Isn't our life wasted in searching for fame and fortune, looking over the truly important things in life such as family and friends? I venture to say that we can all answer yes to many of these things. We might be adults but at heart we are teenagers.

The Bible says that God is a Father, and like the father of the prodigal son, God is waiting with the light on. He is ready and willing to welcome us back home. There is no more reason to stay in our self-imposed pig-pens that we have made for ourselves, no reason to stay since there is nothing left to spend. There are no more friends, no more money, no more time. Now is the time to return home. Now is the time to repent. And that is what repentance is—a change of heart, a true change of life where we turn away from our exiles and turn back to Jesus. Believe me, like any parent, God wants us back home, safe and sound.

Food for Thought

1. Very often we act like teenagers, thinking that we do not need God. We turn away from him and push him out of our life. We go into our "far country" and waste our energy on so many wasteful things. Have you acted like a teenager recently? How have you acted like the younger son in this parable? Did you ever go into a faraway land trying to run away from God? How did this make you feel? How did you return to him?

2. This parable is commonly called the prodigal son. However, some Bible scholars suggested that it should be called the "forgiving father" because the father showed forgiveness to his son. How can we practice forgiveness in our life? Take a few moments and reflect on recent persons or events that have caused you grief. Can you forgive that person? Practicing a lifetime of forgiveness is living in the spirit of the gospel.

3. For further reading: Jonah 4; Matthew 7:13–14; Philippians 4:4–7

DAY 10

In the Groove
MARK 10:32–34

And they were on the road, going up to Jerusalem, and Jesus was walking ahead of them; and they were amazed, and those who followed were afraid. He took the twelve aside again and began to tell them what was to happen to him saying, "See, we are going up to Jerusalem, and the Son of Man will be handed over to the chief priests and the scribes and they will condemn him to death; then they will hand him over to the Gentiles; they will mock him, and spit upon him, and flog him, and kill him; and after three days he will rise again."

There is a concept in psychology called being *in the groove*, which is also referred to as being *in the flow*. Many athletes find themselves in the groove. Take basketball players, for example. Every time the player gets the ball, he makes a basket. Every time he gets the ball, the ball goes through the hoop. It never fails. Game after game, he is on fire, he is *in the groove*.

The same notion applies to writers. An author might write a best-selling novel and follow it up with another great novel. Year after year he keeps producing best sellers. Ideas flow through their head like water flowing down a stream. The author can be said to be *in the groove*.

When the athlete's head is not in the game or the author is not focusing on writing, then they break the flow, they lose concentration, and they falter. If the athlete's head is not focused on the game, he will not perform well. He might get the ball but won't make a basket. If writers easily get distracted they will not produce many books. They are no longer in the groove. Usually their fans forget about them and move onto other books or interesting authors.

In Mark's Gospel we see Jesus in the groove. He knows where he is going. His head is in the game, so to speak. He tells his disciples that he is going to the cross and he even predicts it. He is going to be arrested, mocked, beaten, scourged, killed—and he will be raised on the third day. Jesus is headed for Golgotha and there is no stopping him. The disciples are not really listening to Jesus; they are not in the groove. They are losing their concentration. Jesus warns them about going to the cross, and James and John begin arguing about who will get the best seat in the kingdom! Jesus tells him that even he doesn't have the power to give it to them; it is only for those whom God the Father prepared it from the beginning of the world. The disciples are so off the mark it isn't funny.

Very often we wind up like James and John, worrying and arguing about things that don't really matter. We might worry about our jobs, our future, whether or not our children will get in into a good college. Retirees worry about the future of their Social Security benefits. We are anxious and troubled, worried and concerned about people and events that distract us from the one needful thing, which is following Jesus. There is a beautiful passage in the Gospel of Matthew that I return to every so often throughout the year when life gets hectic and crazy:

"Therefore I tell you, do not worry about your life, what you will eat or what you will drink, or about your body, what you will wear. Is not life more than food, and the body more than clothing? Look at the birds of the air; they neither sow nor reap nor gather into barns, and yet your heavenly Father feeds them. Are you not of more value than they? And can any of you by worrying add a single hour to your span of life? And why do you worry about clothing? Consider the lilies of the field, how they grow; they neither toil nor spin, yet I tell you, even Solomon in all his glory was not clothed like one of these. But if God so clothes the grass of the field, which is alive today and tomorrow is thrown into the oven, will he not much more clothe you—you of little faith? Therefore do not worry, saying, 'What will we eat?' or 'What will we drink?' or 'What will we wear?' For it is the Gentiles who strive for all these things; and indeed your heavenly Father knows that you need all these things. But strive first for the kingdom of God and his righteousness, and all these things will be given to you as well." (Matt 6:25–33)

Jesus reminds his disciples and us that we need to depend on the Lord, not on ourselves. The more we depend on the Lord the less we will get anxious. I am an avid gardener and am amazed that nature finds ways to take care of itself. Birds seem to find worms in my vegetable garden, and sunflowers find places to sprout up from nowhere. Of course, squirrels always find the bird food, especially after I just fill up the birdfeeders! In other words the flowers, birds, and animals seem to just "be" themselves radiating in the glory of God and all of creation.

Discipleship, however, doesn't seem so simple, but it is. Jesus promises us that if we want to be his disciples we have to carry our cross, which means we have to surrender ourselves to him and for him. Taking up our cross means laying down our life for our brother and sister, husband and wife, children and neighbor. It means putting ourself second, being concerned for the needs and cares for the other person rather than on our own needs and wants. If we want to get into the kingdom, and I certainly do, we cannot worry about sitting on Jesus' left or right side. Who cares where we sit in heaven? Getting there is the hard part!

But to get to the kingdom, we have to surrender ourselves to him. How often do we hear about surrendering or sacrifice in our culture and society? Not very often. When do we put ourself second, third, or in fourth place? Corporate America encourages us that if we want to be successful in life we have to step on people's heads, divide and conquer, work hard, and we'll move up the corporate ladder. No one ever remembers the countless athletes who win the bronze medals in the Olympics; we remember the ones who won the gold. How many thousands of nameless authors do we recognize in the local bookstore, yet we seem to know who won the Nobel Prize in literature or the Pulitzer. Our culture puts value on those who get ahead in life who *make it big* and always *get it right*. However, Jesus casts another vision of life. It is okay to get dirty and lay down our life for others. Jesus came not to be served, but to serve, and to give his life as a ransom for many.

Food for Thought

1. The word *humility* comes from the Latin word *humus*, which is the organic material used for gardening; another name for it is compost. When you mix banana peels, eggshells, apple cores, and other organic material together with leaves and dirt, you will eventually get compost. Compost is used as rich organic material for gardens. In our life this means that certain areas need to be broken down, such as our pride, ego, and self-centeredness, so that God's Word can be planted in us, and it will hopefully grow.

2. Try to remember a selfless act of love that you performed for someone else. How did this action make you feel? Did this act inspire others to do similar acts for other people?

3. For further reading: Isaiah 53; Mark 14:65; Luke 18:31–34; Philippians 2:5–11

Day 11

God Doesn't Give Handouts
Mark 8:31–38

Then he began to teach them that the Son of Man must undergo great suffering, and be rejected by the elders, the chief

priests, and the scribes, and be killed, and after three days rise
again. He said all this quite openly. And Peter took him aside
and began to rebuke him. But turning and looking at his dis-
ciples, he rebuked Peter and said, "Get behind me, Satan! For
you are setting your mind not on divine things but on human
things." He called the crowd with his disciples, and said to
them, "If any want to become my followers, let them deny
themselves and take up their cross and follow me."

A few years ago our local newspaper reported that
several teenagers were arrested after stealing a car. The
teens were hanging out late one Friday night and they
were bored, so they broke into a car and decided to take
a joyride. They also managed to break a few laws along
the way. Not only did they break into the car, but they
were caught speeding down the highway. They also got
themselves into a car accident. A mother was driving and
her infant child was in the backseat. Thankfully no one
was hurt. The teenagers fled the scene of the crime by
foot; one of them was eventually caught and arrested.
The mother of the arrested teen told the reporter that she
was sad for the injured mother and her daughter.
However, she also made the point that her son wasn't the
only one who perpetrated the crime. After all, every
teenager across America does stupid things like steal
cars! All teens go for the occasional joyride. Her son was
just caught; most teens get away with it.

The mother of the teen was blaming society and culture for her son's predicament. She did not take responsibility for her son's actions. Her story is revealing for
many reasons. Not once did she admit to the reporter that

her son committed five serious crimes and nearly killed two innocent people in that seemingly innocent joyride. But it also shows the lack of responsibility and accountability in our culture. How many people blame others for their life's troubles? How often have you heard someone say, "Someone else made me do it"? Even as early as the beginning of the Book of Genesis, people were blaming each other for their bad situation. When Eve ate the fruit of the tree of the knowledge of good and evil, she gave some fruit to Adam, and he ate it. When God found out that Eve ate of the fruit, he inquired of them why they did so. Adam's first response was that Eve made me do it. Eve said that the serpent made her do it. So the blame game started very early. People always blame others for their own problems.

People often blame others for their actions, especially in our country where handouts are given out in the form of free clothes, shelter, or food. A handout is supposed to be a hand *up*, a short-term answer to a long-term need. People need free food to get them through the week, but they ultimately need a job so that they can go out and purchase food for themselves. People need a roof over their head, but they eventually need a job to pay for the house themselves. Our society does not help citizens survive on their own. If you continue giving handouts, people will never learn what it takes to get a hand up and begin to be accountable for their life and the lives of those around them.

Jesus came not to give us a divine handout, but to give us a hand *up*, a hand up from our falling so far down the so-called spiritual ladder that we hit bottom. The cross is not God's form of social welfare but his way of total and complete responsibility. God is tired of giving handouts. For centuries he was giving away freebies. He fed Israel manna in the wilderness. After a while they started complaining because they did not like the manna. They expected different food occasionally. He sent them prophets to preach his Word. They expected him to send more prophets. He gave them the law written on tablets so they could read and understand them. Finally, God was tired of giving freebies because his chosen people were not acting responsibly. They kept complaining and arguing with him. Just open up to any place in the Old Testament and you will see grumbling, complaining, and arguing about how God is treating them. Israel acted like spoiled children always wanting more cookies and milk, even though God gave them dozens of cookies.

This time God wanted to teach us the true meaning of responsibility, so he sent his Son. Jesus was the only person who was completely and totally responsible. It was not easy though. In the Gospel of Mark Jesus fervently prays in the garden of Gethsemane to let the cup pass from him, which is another way of saying, Let the cross pass; don't make me take it. But at the end of the prayer he says, But not my will, but as *you* will, Lord. Three times he prays this prayer to God the Father. Mark shows us that Jesus is truly human. He wants to let this cross pass from him, but in the end he confesses that God's will be done, no matter what the consequences were. Upon the third time that Jesus recited the prayer, Judas enters the garden with a band of Jewish soldiers to arrest him.

The cross is a symbol of God's divine hand *up*, not a handout. Sure, the world isn't perfect. Yes, people mess up their lives, sometimes in big ways. Yes, teenagers steal cars and get into accidents and nearly kill people. But Jesus wants us to take up our cross and follow him. Take up your life with all its problems and cares, concerns and troubles, and follow. For once, just once, take responsibility and be accountable for your life, not pointing fingers, blaming, or complaining to others.

Food for Thought

1. Are there times when you blamed other people for your actions even though it may have been totally unfounded?

2. How can you take more responsibility regarding your own spirituality? What are some of the spiritual practices that might help you take better responsibility of your life?

3. What are the crosses in your life today? How can you carry these crosses in faith?

4. For further reading: Mark 13; and 1 Corinthians 1:18–25

DAY 12

Blessed Is He Who Comes in the Name of the Lord
JOHN 12:12–17

The next day the great crowd that had come to the festival heard that Jesus was coming to Jerusalem. So they took branches of palm trees and went out to meet him shouting, "Hosanna! Blessed is the one who comes in the name of the Lord—the King of Israel!" Jesus found a young donkey and sat on it; as it is written: "Do not be afraid, daughter of Zion. Look, your king is coming, sitting on a donkey's colt!" His disciples did not understand these things at first; but when Jesus was glorified, then they remembered that these things had been done to him.

A week before Easter, Christians from around the world celebrate Holy Week. During Holy Week we follow Jesus throughout the end of his earthly journey: the commemoration of the Last Supper with his disciples, his betrayal and arrest in the garden of Gethsemane, his trial before Pontius Pilate, his beatings and crucifixion, and finally on the joyous day of Easter his rising from the dead. These last events of Jesus' life are recorded in the gospels in slightly different ways. When you have some free time, it would be a very good spiritual exercise to read each of the four gospel accounts of Jesus' passion, death, and resurrection. The passages are not very long. This would give you a better picture of how Christians have viewed Jesus' death.

Very often, Holy Week precedes or coincides with the Jewish festival of Passover, which is a festal period recalling the Israelites being saved from the Egyptians. Every year for thousands of years, Jews have gathered during this solemn time to remember the great things that the Lord has done for them. The Jews have a special Passover dinner called a Seder, which includes many different types of food: lamb shanks, bitter herbs, unleavened bread, honey, and wine. The youngest son in the house inquires of the father, "Why is this night different from all other nights?" And the father responds with a brief explanation of the Exodus story. The family follows a prayer book called the Haggadah, which contains the scriptural references to the Passover event. I once had the wonderful opportunity to join an ecumenical Passover Seder and it was very moving. Every dish has a symbolic meaning, and the scripture readings and prayers are very meaningful.

Jesus sent his disciples into Jerusalem in order to celebrate the Passover meal. The Passover was a special festal celebration in Judaism and it commemorated the Israelites exodus out of Egypt. The Jews were in bondage and slavery to Pharaoh so God sent them Moses to lead them out of Egypt with a pillar of cloud by night and a pillar of fire by day. Every year they were commanded to eat a special meal in commemoration of this salvific event. The Passover was not just an ordinary meal, but included memories of oppression and salvation, slavery, freedom, exile, and deliverance. Every year at the feast of Passover Jews remembered their bondage to Pharaoh and their subsequent deliverance out of Egypt. These strong memories were of course present at Jesus' last Passover with his disciples, what we call the Last Supper.

Jerusalem would have been full of pilgrims coming to the city for the feast. Their tensions would have been high. People would have been buying food as well as material goods for their travel. Lambs, herbs, and bread were the basis for the Passover meal, and of course wine. All of this information serves as the background for Palm Sunday. The Gospel of John tells us that Jesus rides into the city on a donkey, fulfilling the prophecy from Zachariah: "Do not be afraid, daughter of Zion. Look, your king is coming, sitting on a donkey's colt!"

Jesus fulfills this prophecy as he humbly enters into Jerusalem on a donkey, a beast of burden. An earthly king would have entered the city riding on horses or riding on a chariot with a military procession, showing his power and might. In our society, a governor or president would enter the city in a long limousine procession with police cars and secret service personnel around the motorcade. Television and media vans would probably follow. However, Jesus enters the city in a very quiet and humble manner, although the crowds want to make him a king as they put out palm branches.

This same crowd who greets Jesus in the city, giving him praise, would later turn on him when he was crucified. The crowd that exclaims *Hosanna* later exclaims *Crucify him, crucify him*. At first this reaction might seem strange but it shows the wavering of humanity, that the crowds can be either for you or against you, depending on their emotions. The crowds are certainly fickle; sometimes they want to make Jesus king and at other times they want to stone him.

You might be wondering what Passover has to do with Palm Sunday. During that first Palm Sunday people like you and me were holding palm branches and standing in the streets, crying "Hosanna, blessed is he who comes in the name of the Lord." Hosanna means *save us*. As Jesus entered Jerusalem, the memory of the first Passover was in their minds and on their hearts. Memories of slavery and bitter bondage to the Egyptians, their cries to the Lord, the help of Moses, their escape into the wilderness, and their being saved from the Egyptian armies. As the crowds welcomed Jesus into Jerusalem, they were welcoming their savior — one greater than Moses. They were welcoming their king into their life. Jesus was not just another Moses, but one greater than Moses. Moses led his people to the Promised Land, the land flowing with milk and honey. But the Promised Land that Jesus is leading us to is not Canaan; neither is it the earthly Jerusalem, but the Jerusalem from above, the kingdom of God. We call this the New Jerusalem, where there is no more pain, no more sickness, no more cancer, no more terrorism, no more fighting, no more wars, no more division, just pure love, joy, and peace. This is the Promised Land that Jesus leads us to. He is in front paving the way, and all we have to do is to follow him. But we are not there yet; we are still in the wilderness, wandering around, trying to find our own way.

If you ever traveled to the southwestern United States, you know what I am talking about. The desert wilderness is not some lush green forest with a bunch of lakes and mountains. The wilderness that I am talking about is a large, dry, hot, ragged, and rocky place with little water and a lot of heat. Danger lurks everywhere: snakes, scorpions, tarantulas, bobcats, and mountain lions. The desert is vast and hot; there is very little water and shade. Desert conditions are treacherous and can be deadly if you are not prepared.

Our life is a type of spiritual desert. We find ourselves in a vast spiritual wasteland where there is very little life. It is vast and dry; we have trouble finding the quiet waters of rest and comfort. We are barraged and attacked by many trials, temptations, and troubles. If we are not careful, we will get lost in this spiritual desert. However, if we focus on Jesus we can follow him to the oasis of life. Jesus is our Good Shepherd, who like Moses before him leads us to the Promised Land. Jesus will not fail us. He feeds us with the Bread of Life, which is his Word. He gives us his own Living Waters when we thirst. He comforts us when we get scared. All we have to do is follow him, step by step until we reach that Promised Land where we will feast forever in the kingdom, where we will have everlasting peace, love, and joy forever and ever.

Food for Thought

1. Have you ever had a spiritual "desert experience" as was described earlier in this chapter? What was the context of this experience? How did it make you feel?

2. Very often, when we find ourselves in a spiritual desert, we feel lonely and out of touch with others. However, we are not alone; the

Lord watches over us each and every day. Right now, in some monastery, parish, or convent, people are praying for you and me. Maybe you can find solace in the fact that we are all connected through prayer.

3. For further reading: Psalm 3; Psalm 136; Exodus 13:1–10; Matthew 21:1–11

DAY: 13

How Do You Read?
ROMANS 15:4–6

For whatever was written in former days was written for our instruction, so that by steadfastness and by the encouragement of the scriptures we might have hope. May the God of steadfastness and encouragement grant you to live in harmony with one another, in accordance with Christ Jesus, so that together you may with one voice glorify the God and Father of our Lord Jesus Christ.

I fondly remember our summer family vacations as we traveled up and down the Eastern seaboard, learning about the diverse and rich history of the various towns and cities, as well as sampling a wide variety of foods as we journeyed along the way. Nothing is better than blueberry pie in New England or an Eastern Carolina pulled-pork BBQ sandwich or fresh Maryland she-crab soup —

which, strange as it is, is its actual name. One thing is certain; no matter where we went, we always ate well!

Vacations are not without setbacks, no matter how minor they may seem to be — Dad getting lost while driving, the flat tire that happens during a rainstorm, or a package of crayons found melted to the car seat! Of course, there is the usual spat between siblings as well as cries of "Are we there yet?" that are repeated like a funeral dirge again and again until the car rolls to its final resting place. Yet the entire travel experience provides colorful moments in the collective memory of families, which children can pass onto their children and grandchildren.

One summer vacation particularly sticks out in my mind. I remember that it was ungodly hot; anyone who has been to DC during the summer knows that the heat and humidity are stifling. I remember visiting a big white building near the center of the city. At the time, I didn't know the exact significance of the building. Only later did I come to find out that it was the Capitol. We waited in a very long line that snaked and meandered around the front stairs. We waited and waited and waited. I thought that they must have been selling ice cream or hot dogs, judging from this very long line! But as we slowly made it to the front of the line, I noticed a large open space underneath the tall wide dome in the center of the building. There were two armed guards standing on either side of a square wooden table and people smiling and taking pictures of something below them. As we approached, I saw what everyone was looking at: two large glass cases with yellowish paper. I had no idea why everyone was smiling and taking pictures and talking. To me, these were just words on a piece of paper. Only later did I realize that these two pieces of paper were the Declaration of Independence and the Constitution of the United States. There was a special exhibit taking place in Washington and these documents were out for public display.

Every year millions of immigrants come to the United States because of these two pieces of paper. They may think they are coming because of good jobs, better financial compensation, good housing, or improved education for their children. But deep down they are coming to our country because of the freedoms guaranteed in these two documents: the freedom to work wherever one wants to work, the freedom to live and to play, the freedom to worship as they see fit. So much of our life depends on these two documents. These two documents form and shape the laws of our country and our lives, so much so that we don't even think about it. We go about our daily routines without thinking about these two pieces of paper.

We also forget that some people spend their entire lives studying, reading, debating, and arguing over the words in these documents. Lawyers and judges commit themselves to understand what these words mean and how they affect the country. The judges of the Supreme Court spend their careers interpreting and understanding how these documents work and that the laws that our government creates does not hinder or detract from the rights, freedoms, and privileges contained in these documents.

Well, the Bible is to Christians what the Declaration of Independence and the Constitution are to our government. At first glance the Bible may just seem like words on a page, many words in fact, too many for some of us. Stories of intrigue, murder, war, love, hate, anger, theft, and history fill its pages. The Bible includes different forms of literature such as poetry, genealogies, parables, and so forth. The Bible is comprised not just words about God or what we think about God, but the very Word of God himself. When we read the Bible, we are hearing God speak to us. Now that is truly awesome!

Therefore, it is very important to study, read, and interpret this Word. Just as the Declaration of Independence and the Constitution form and shape our way of life here in the United States, so too does the Word of God form and shape our life. Christians gather each Sunday and hear this Word, which is lived out in their local faith communities. This Word feeds and nourishes us from week to week and from season to season.

However, we also need to hand down this Word to the next generation. After all, Paul reminds us in his Letter to the Romans that we have been instructed in God's Word and are supposed to hand down this instruction to our children and to our children's children. If we don't hand it down, how are they going to know it? More importantly, how are they going to live a Christ-centered life if they don't know about the Word of God? They will know it only if we teach them! The Apostle Paul didn't learn the Word through osmosis, but took great pains to read, study, interpret, and yes, sometimes argue about it. But he made the effort. If lawyers and judges spend so much of their time studying and learning about the Constitution, perhaps we ought to spend some extra time with God's Word, in prayer and study.

Christians need to be just as diligent and regular about reading scripture as lawyers and judges read and study the Declaration of Independence and the Constitution. I often visit people in my parish. Some of them have Bibles on their coffee tables, and many of them are well worn. Of course, seeing this makes me happy. What doesn't make me happy are the Bibles that look like they were just purchased yesterday from the bookstore. They sit there on the coffee table, sometimes collecting dust. They are never opened. Many Christians suffer from a terrible disease called DBS: Dusty Bible Syndrome. They have a Bible but never read it! Reading and studying the Word of God is a task that will bring you joy. When you read about God's wonderful work in the world, in creating the world, in saving the Israelites from the Egyptians, sending the prophets to bring the Israelites back to repentance, and then finally sending his Son into our life, you will see that God's word is dynamic, encouraging, and life-giving. I hope that you will appreciate the Bible and turn to it regularly throughout the course of your life. You won't be disappointed.

Food for Thought

1. Many Christians suffer from Dusty Bible Syndrome. Do you or someone in your family have DBS? You might want to think about what deters you from reading the Bible more often.

2. One way to study the Word of God is get involved in a local prayer group or Bible study group sponsored by a local parish. When more

than one person gets involved, it requires accountability and responsibility. Try to find a Bible study group in your area. You can search your local newspaper or ask your pastor for assistance.

3. There are numerous Bible study aides available in both print and electronic forms that can assist you in studying the scriptures, such as single or multivolume Bible commentaries, Bible dictionaries, and Bible concordances. Take some time and learn more about the Bible.

4. For further reading: Deuteronomy 5:1–27; Psalm 119; Romans 10:14–21; 1 Timothy 4:11–16

DAY 14

Jesus Irritates Me!
MARK 5:1–20

They came to the other side of the sea, to the country of the Gerasenes. And when he had stepped out of the boat, immediately a man out of the tombs with an unclean spirit met him. He lived among the tombs; and no one could restrain him any more, even with a chain; for he had often been restrained with shackles and chains, but the chains he wrenched apart, and the shackles he broke in pieces; and no one had the strength to subdue him. Night and day among the tombs and on the mountains he was always howling and bruising himself with stones. When he saw Jesus from a distance, he ran and bowed down before him.

I have to make a public confession: Jesus, the Son of God, the Son of the Virgin Mary, the cousin of John the Baptist, the One who calmed the storms and who walked on water, irritates me. Actually, he irritates me really bad. As difficult or as embarrassing to admit, it is true.

This irritation is like poison ivy in the summertime. There is nothing worse than getting poison ivy in the summertime. First you see a few red bumps on your skin, which you think are mosquito bites. And then you begin scratching. The more you scratch, the more it itches. The more it itches, the more you scratch. The next thing you know is that the small patch of poison ivy has spread down your leg. Mosquito bites are also irritating. They bite you all over your body, and then you lay there in bed scratching away.

Other things in life irritate me, too. I cannot stand red lights. So much of our life is wasted sitting in traffic, waiting for a light to turn green. Or what about waiting in a doctor's office? Now that can also be irritating. Waiting and waiting for that nurse to open the door and to call out your name. You sit there reading a book or a magazine, playing Sudoku or a crossword puzzle, or even falling asleep, just waiting for a doctor these days. The list goes on and on. I'm sure that you can find many other things in life that you find irritating—I know that I can.

When reading the scriptures, we see that Jesus irritated a bunch of people. Actually, Jesus seems to irritate everyone he meets. Even when Jesus was not yet old

enough to talk, let alone walk, he irritated King Herod.
Herod was the king of Judea and when he found out that
Jesus was born, he got so mad that he had all the children
in Bethlehem killed who were two years old and younger,
just to protect his own kingly throne. Jesus also irritated
Mary and Joseph when he was in the Temple, teaching
the scribes and elders, and his parents couldn't find him.

There are other occasions when the Jewish leaders
tried to entrap Jesus in his words. One time when Jesus
was preaching, people around him picked up stones in
order to kill him. Other time entire crowds wanted to
throw Jesus off a cliff. But why was this meek, mild,
humble, forgiving, and merciful Jesus so irritating? Well,
Jesus always told the truth and he certainly did not sugar
coat it! He came straight out and said that a sin is a sin,
but because God the Father is loving and kind, he will
offer forgiveness. Jesus told the Jews that while it was
good to follow the commandments, the rule of love was
greater. What good is following the 613 legal codes if they
could not actually love other people? They didn't like to
hear this, of course. Jesus irritated them big time!

When Jesus entered the area of the Gerasenes, sometimes called the Gadarenes, he ticked off an entire village.
Mark tells us that Jesus was on the other side of the Sea of
Galilee when he met a demoniac who lived among the
tombs in a non-Jewish area. Jesus drove the demons out
of the possessed man and into a herd of swine, who then
ran down into the sea and drowned. After being cured, the
formerly possessed men made a confession of faith that
Jesus was the Son of God. But the local people reacted
negatively. They wanted Jesus out of their lives for good.

Why were they unhappy? Because even though the possessed man was now cured, raising pigs was an essential component of the local economy. Jesus came along and upset their way of life, their cultural procedures and rules, and revealed that he was truly the Son of God, the one who brings wholeness and completeness to a fallen creation.

When I was younger, this particular reading from Mark always bothered me. It brought up images from horror stories, movies like *The Omen*, *The Exorcist*, or *The Amityville Horror*—tales of demon-possessed children or adults spitting up vomit and blood, and who are locked in closets or terrifying neighborhoods. Most of what we think or know about demon possession is from Hollywood movies, which are always full of props and special effects. But if we take a close look around us, we will quickly see how much of life is polluted by the work of people serving evil desires or temptations. Daily tales of terror, abduction, drug overdose, murders, suicides, extortion, not to mention, of course, white-collar crime and sexual misconduct bombard us through television, radio, and the Internet. Our modern evils are really not much different. We just have to pay closer attention and open our eyes to the reality that there is a constant battle going on in our lives between Jesus Christ and Satan who, as the Apostle Paul reminds us, comes clothed as an angel of light, trying to deceive us from following Jesus.

One would think that when Jesus healed the demon-possessed man that his friends and fellow townspeople would have been happy. After all, their friend who was once possessed by demons was now healed and in his right mind. Even though their herd of pigs was sacrificed, their friend was in much better shape. But what did they do? Did they throw a party for Jesus and their friends? No, they threw Jesus out of their village. They actually threw the Son of God out of their lives! Can you imagine? These villagers were so angry with Jesus because he helped their friend, but they were more worried about their pigs! Jesus must have really irritated those people.

If we are honest with ourselves and listen to the gospel, we might find that Jesus' words strike a cord in our hearts that we might find irritating, too. I know that even though Jesus wants me to love other people, I find it hard, even impossible to love people all of the time. And Jesus reminds me to be forgiving and merciful, and in my heart of hearts I want to get revenge. Yes, Jesus is irritating, just like the prophets of the Old Testament were irritating; especially the prophets like Jeremiah, Amos, Hosea, and Ezekiel. They too were thrown out of towns and villages and attacked on more than one occasion for speaking the truth. Yet they spoke on God's behalf. I guess this gospel message will irritate most of us; it should irritate us to do something about it. Perhaps if we get very irritated it might lead us to change our lives, or at least, to have our lives changed. If we have an open heart and want to hear the gospel, our lives will certainly be changed forever. If not, maybe we need to ask ourselves, whose message are we listening to anyway?

Some scholars assume that demonic possession in the ancient world can be attributed to mental illness, such as schizophrenia. Many of the symptoms or manifestations of mental disorders may mimic what people think of as demon possession: harming themselves or those people around them, speaking to someone who is not really there, or some other behavior. Modern medicine tells us that mental disorders can now be treated with drugs to create a sense of normal lifestyle for those people who are afflicted with such problems. However, while this may be true, we cannot discount demonic possession as a reality. Christians believe that Jesus Christ is the Lord over all creation, but we also know that evil exists in this world. The high rates of physical, emotional, and verbal abuse; the nonstop warfare, terrorism, and drug addiction; not to mention political corruption and other inhumane activities—all are evil actions and need to be named in order for us to fight against them.

Food for Thought

1. When reading the gospels, have you ever thought that Jesus was irritating? If so, how?

2. If we are comfortable with Jesus, maybe we are not reading the gospels with an open heart. It is easy to miss the message if we are reading into the Bible our own ideas and thoughts. If we read the gospel with an open mind and heart, we will feel just a bit uncomfortable because it is not always easy or convenient to turn the other cheek or to love people who really bother us, but that is in fact what the gospels say.

3. For further reading: Matthew 23; Luke 4:21–30; John 6:1–15

DAY 15
Don't Be Late for Dinner
MATTHEW 22:1–4

Once more Jesus spoke to them in parables, saying: "The kingdom of heaven may be compared to a king who gave a wedding banquet for his son. He sent his slaves to call those who had been invited to the wedding banquet, but they would not come. Again he sent other slaves, saying, 'Tell those who have been invited: Look, I have prepared my dinner, my oxen and my fat calves have been slaughtered, and everything is ready; come to the wedding banquet.'"

There once was a couple who moved into a new neighborhood. They unpacked all of their boxes, decorated their house, and put everything in order. Now, they were ready to meet the other neighbors on the block. So they decided that they would invite one couple per week for Sunday night dinner. They would have a nice meal and spend time talking and sharing about their neighborhood, their families, and their friends. So, they set out for their new adventure. They invited a couple from down the street. They planned their menu complete with hors d'oeuvres and drinks, salad, entrée, and dessert. It was such a wonderful evening. The two couples talked about work, their children, and about life in general. Before leaving, the host told the couple what a wonderful time everyone had and that they were always welcome to come back. "Our house is your house," he said.

The same thing happened the following week. Another couple came over and they again had a great meal, hors d'oeuvres and drinks, salad, entrée, and dessert. Again, everyone had a great time talking about their children, about their work, and about life in general. At the end of the meal the host said what a wonderful time everyone had and that they were always welcome back. "Our house is your house," he said. The same thing happened week three and week four.

After the fourth couple came over, the host couple was tired and wanted a break from having guests, at least for several weeks. They decided that after a few weeks they would resume their routine of hosting a dinner party for the neighbors. So on Sunday night the couple decided to have a simple meal of grilled cheese and tomato soup. They ate alone, so they thought. During the middle of dinner the doorbell rang. This was odd since no one usually came around on Sunday evening except for the couples whom they previously invited for supper. The husband inquired of his wife, "Are you expecting anyone?" She responded, "No, are you expecting anyone?" He said "No." So the husband got up from the table, went over to the door, opened it. Before him were the three couples who had previously come over for dinner, each holding a bottle of wine, flowers, and a box of chocolates. The husband thought this was strange but offered a courteous, "Hello, how are you?" The couples responded likewise and returned the smile. There was a nervous moment and everyone stood in complete silence. Then all of a sudden the husband inquired, "Please forgive me, but what are you doing here? It's late and it's Sunday night and we are

very tired from a long day of Church and yard-work."
They all responded in unison, "The last time we were here
for dinner you told us that we were always welcome for
dinner. You also said that your house is our house!" The
man looked at them and said, "Gee, I guess you're right. I
did say that, didn't I?" He then invited them in and said,
"I hope you don't mind grilled cheese and soup!"

At one time or another we probably have all said,
"Our house is your house," and "Please come back anytime for dinner," but we usually say this out of social eti-
quette or to be friendly and warm with our family and
friends. Deep down we actually do mean what we are
saying, but on the surface we also know that people generally do not take us literally. If we invite someone over
for Sunday dinner one week, we do not expect them to
pop in again the following Sunday!

However, contrary to this couple in this story, our
Lord does expect us to pop in to visit him at his house,
which is the Church. After all, don't we call the Church
"the house of God?" God's house is our house and we are
invited to dinner week after week after week—and the
Lord certainly means what he says. He wants us to come
and sit at his table and feast on the food of eternal life.
The Gospel of John refers to Jesus as the *Bread of Life*
who feeds and nourishes us with his teaching and his broken body and his spilled blood as we hear our priest
exclaim each Sunday, "Take and eat. This is my body
which is broken for you" and "Drink of it all of you. This
is my blood of the new testament which is shed for you
for the remission of sins." Jesus' teaching and his body
and blood sustain us throughout the week, and we return

back to be fed again. He leads us to the still waters to drink of the Water of Life. His words provide comfort and encouragement during difficult times. They lead us back to the narrow path when we go astray. They instill contrition in our hearts when we are guilty of wrongdoing.

One of Jesus' parables is about a king who gives a marriage feast for his son. In antiquity, weddings were not only religious events but cultural and social ones as well. Marriages often became the bonds that joined warring families together, increased one's wealth and security, and were also a sign of continuity as the children from the couple would hopefully carry on the family name for the next generation. Marriages involved great festivities, including lots of food and of course wine. The Gospel of John contains a reference to the wedding at Cana of Galilee where Jesus and his mother were invited. We are not given specific details but it is here at Cana where Jesus performed his first miracle by turning water into wine (John 2:1–11).

However, Matthew tells us a parable about another wedding. Here, the king invites his friends to the banquet feast for his son, yet the persons who were invited did not come. Then he sends his servants out to the very same people and tries to compel them by saying, "I have made ready my dinner, my oxen and fat calves are killed, and everything is ready; come to the marriage feast" (Matt 22:4). Some of the guests make excuses and leave while the rest of the guests harm the servants and kill them. The king then sends his troops and soldiers to destroy them and burn down their city. Then the king tells his servants to go to the thoroughfares and invite others in, both the bad and the good, so the wedding will be full. However, one of the guests does not have the proper wedding attire and is seized by the king and thrown out of the party, as Matthew says, "Bind him hand and foot, and cast him into the outer darkness; there will be weeping and gnashing of teeth. For many are called but few are chosen" (Matt 22:12–14).

This parable reminds us that the kingdom of heaven is akin to a wedding feast to which the king, who is God the Father, invites us. However, we are not only called to respond to the wedding feast, but also to be prepared for it—in the case of the parable, to have our wedding garment ready. In the ancient world, wedding guests were typically given a special outer garment with which they wore for the wedding celebration and feast that followed. It is one thing that this man found himself in the feast but quite another when the king saw that he wasn't prepared. Yet, I think the same holds true today. It would be very strange if we went to a wedding ceremony where the women and men were wearing beautiful gowns and tuxedos, where there were nicely decorated tables with flowers and tablecloths, and delicious food and drinks, and then one person walked in with a tank-top, shorts, and sandals, wearing a baseball cap. I'm sure most people would at least look askance at this person. Surely the person would be asked to leave or at least put on proper attire for the wedding reception. While the person might have an invitation, clearly they would not be dressed or prepared for the occasion.

The parable is also a reminder that those who were originally invited to the feast did not come, so the king invited those who were far off, or as Matthew says earlier in his gospel, "I tell you, many will come from east and west and will eat with Abraham and Isaac and Jacob in the kingdom of heaven, while the heirs of the kingdom will be thrown into the outer darkness, where there will be weeping and gnashing of teeth" (Matt 8:11–14). We also have very similar sayings in the gospel: "The Son of Man will send his angels, and they will collect out of his kingdom all causes of sin and all evildoers, and throw them into the furnace of fire; there will be weeping and gnashing of teeth. Then the righteous will shine like the sun in the kingdom of their Father. Let anyone with ears listen!" (Matt 13:41–43).

One of the images of the kingdom of heaven is the wedding banquet. In the Book of Revelation we are told that at the end of time, after all the wars, tribulation, destruction, and rebellion take place, Jesus, who is referred to as the Lamb of God, will come down from heaven seated on his throne, with all his angels and all his power and all his might, and he will be dressed like a beautiful bridegroom who is awaiting his bride. The bride is the Church, adorned in all beauty and splendor, just like a bride is dressed on her wedding day. And then the marriage feast of the Lamb will take place, a feast of feasts, and everyone is invited to the supper. However, we have to make sure that we have our wedding garment preserved in purity. Our baptismal garment becomes our wedding garment, our ticket into the kingdom. If we do not have a wedding garment, we will not be able to join the party; the man in the parable did not have a wedding garment and was thrown out of the banquet to where men will weep and gnash their teeth. Matthew reminds us that the Lord means what he says; he keeps his end of the bargain even if we do not keep ours.

There was a small parish that called a new pastor to lead them. They were so happy to have a young, educated pastor to help them grow and do the Lord's work in their community. The first week the pastor gave a great sermon and everyone was pleased. Following the Sunday service, they greeted the pastor and told them that they were pleased that he accepted to serve at their small parish. The second week the pastor delivered the same sermon. The people were still happy that they had a new pastor and didn't mind that he repeated the same sermon from the previous week. Again, on the third Sunday the pastor delivered the same sermon. The parish was now wondering if this guy was a dud; after all, he delivered the same sermon three Sundays in a row. The parish council decided to talk to their pastor about his lack of performance in the pulpit. So, after the third week, during the coffee social, the parish council met with the pastor. They said how wonderful he was and how they enjoyed his family and were so pleased that he accepted their call to come to their community. However, the council confessed to him that they were upset that he gave the same sermon three weeks in a row. Smiling he looked at them and said, "I'll change my sermon when you start listening!"

In the same way, gospel stories are repetitive for a reason; perhaps we are not listening to what the gospels are telling us. We tend to hear what we want to hear and forget the rest. We pick and choose bits and pieces of the gospel rather than hearing and accepting the entire gospel message as a whole. Today we are once again invited to hear the gospel call to faith, striving to preserve our baptismal garment white as snow, so that we will one day be invited to sit at the table of the Lord, for the most delicious dinner of all, the wedding banquet of the kingdom.

Food for Thought

1. The gospels tell us that Jesus fed the 5,000 with five loaves of bread and two fish. He also changed water into wine. And the Gospel of John refers to him as the *bread of life*. Think about the many ways that Jesus feeds you in your daily walk of faith. Furthermore, how can you in turn help to feed others, both physically and spiritually?

2. One of my friends said that when he reads the Bible, he is spending time with Jesus. Do you spend time with Jesus by reading his Word? If you are pressed for time and cannot devote time to reading the Bible, how about listening to the Bible on compact disk while driving or while doing your chores at home?

3. For further reading: Mark 8:1–10; Luke 14:16–24; Revelation 21

DAY 16

My Ways Are Not Your Ways
MARK 15:33–39

When it was noon, darkness came over the whole land until three in the afternoon. At three o'clock Jesus cried out with a loud voice, "Eloi, Eloi, lema sabachthani?" which means, "My God, my God, why have you forsaken me?" When some of the bystanders heard it, they said, "Listen, he is calling for Elijah." And someone ran, filled a sponge with sour wine, put it on a stick, and gave it to him to drink, saying, "Wait, let us see whether Elijah will come to take him down." Then Jesus gave a loud cry and breathed his last. And the curtain of the temple was torn in two, from top to bottom. Now when the centurion, who stood facing him, saw that in this way he breathed his last, he said, "Truly this man was God's Son!"

Late night one Saturday night at 11:30 p.m. in Charlotte, North Carolina, a 911 call went out from the Timber Creek apartment complex, which is not too far from our parish community. It was a 911 call like the many routine 911 calls that the police receive every night. Two officers responded to the call, which happened to be a domestic dispute. It was a routine call like the other calls police receive every day; one call among many. However, this phone call proved to be different, because a local street thug, who has been in and out of jail and in and out of trouble for years, approached the two officers from behind and shot them in the back of the head, exe-

cution style. Two shots, *bang — bang*. The officers did not
have time to pull their weapons. They were shot dead on
the spot. One officer left behind a wife, a two-year-old
son, and an unborn child. The other officer also left
behind a wife and an extended family. The street thug sits
in jail while the families of the dead officers mourn for
their loved ones.

People in the community have been asking: Why did
this awful tragedy take place? During the week following
the killings, the media, neighborhood associations, and
schools have been asking the same question: Why did this
take place? What if the school system had done a better
job educating this low-life, petty criminal? Maybe he
wouldn't have turned to a life of crime. What if we had
stronger gun control laws? Maybe these officers wouldn't
have been shot in the first place. What if his parents were
more active in his life and showed him love? Maybe he
wouldn't have been so angry and wouldn't have turned to
a life of street crime. The questions go on and on and on.

For centuries people have asked similar questions
about the death of Jesus. What if Judas hadn't betrayed
Jesus? Maybe Jesus wouldn't have been arrested. What
if Peter and the other apostles were armed with swords
and clubs and used force to protect Jesus? Maybe Jesus
wouldn't have been killed. What if Pontius Pilate was
kinder and refused to hand Jesus over to the Jews? For
centuries, people have asked these questions. But the fact
remains: Jesus Christ, the Son of God, was arrested, put
on trial, and died a very public, shameful, and humiliat-
ing death on the cross, outside of Jerusalem on a Friday
afternoon. How could this have happened? How could

God have allowed this to happen? Why did Jesus have to die this way?

We might find an answer in the words of the prophet Isaiah. Isaiah was a great prophet in the Old Testament and told the Israelites about God and about repentance. In Isaiah chapter 55, we hear the following words: "For my thoughts are not your thoughts, nor are your ways my ways, says the LORD. For as the heavens are higher than the earth, so are my ways higher than your ways, and my thoughts than your thoughts" (Isa 55:8–9)."

Apparently, Isaiah is telling us that God does not think and act like we do. We cannot guess what is on God's mind or what he is up to. God is totally other. God allowed his only begotten Son to be handed over to Herod and Pilate and to die a shameful death on the cross. How may parents would allow their children to go and play out on the highway in front of cars or to play with a handgun or to put their children in direct danger—no one, right? But God the Father allowed his only begotten Son to be bruised and humiliated. Jesus Christ, the Good Shepherd, who showed love, peace, mercy, and forgiveness, was taken outside the city gates and hung on a cross, and Isaiah's voice echoes, "My ways are not your ways, and my thoughts are not your thoughts."

When we see Jesus on a crucifix, we stare at his dead cold body hanging on a piece of wood. We remember the beatings, the mocking, the nails, and the pain. We remember the emptiness and the emotions that his mother and his disciples must have felt. We remember the thorns and the robe. We remember the yelling and the screaming. We remember the sadness. An Orthodox Christian theologian,

Paul Evdokimov, said that God shows his absurd love to the world through the crucifixion of Jesus. The cross is indeed absurd. It was the common form of criminal punishment during those times, and yet it is through the cross that God shows his love to the world. The cross is not the way that I would choose or most likely you would choose, but it is the way that God chose to do it. As Isaiah said, "My ways are not your ways, and my thoughts are not your thoughts." God goes against every bit of human logic and rational thinking in order to show us that he indeed loves us.

We live in an absurd world, a world where thousands of street thugs grow up in poverty and learn a life of crime. We live in a world in which handguns proliferate and find their way into the hands of teenagers. We live in a world in which drugs, prostitution, crime, hatred, anger, and prejudice reign. We live in a world in which young police officers, the very people who protect and care for us, are gunned down in cold blood. Both the cross and the world are indeed absurd. Yet it is through this very imperfect and absurd world that God shows his perfect love through the cross of Christ. And it is this message of the cross that we are called to follow. Christians everywhere are called once again to share the perfect love, peace, and humility of the cross in this very imperfect world in which we live.

Food for Thought

1. God's ways are certainly not our ways. Have you ever prayed for something or someone

and never received an answer that you expected? How did that make you feel? Did you give up praying or did you persist with faith, persistence, and trust?

2. Have you ever lived through a tragic event such as a robbery, car accident, or other trauma? What were the details of the event? How did you get through it? What were the outcomes?

3. When we pray the Lord's Prayer we say, "Thy will be done." We always pray that the Lord's will is done in our life. Take a few moments and reflect on the Lord's Prayer, especially this important petition. How can we better do the Lord's will in our life?

4. For further reading: Isaiah 53; Psalm 22; Acts 1; Philippians 2:5–11

DAY 17

Finding God in Narnia
MATTHEW 5:1–11

When Jesus saw the crowds, he went up the mountain; and after he sat down, his disciples came to him. Then he began to speak, and taught them, saying:

"Blessed are the poor in spirit, for theirs is the kingdom of heaven. Blessed are those who mourn, for they will be comforted. Blessed are the meek, for they will inherit the earth. Blessed are those who hunger and thirst for righteousness, for they will be filled. Blessed are the merciful, for they will receive mercy. Blessed are the pure in heart, for they will see God. Blessed are the peacemakers, for they will be called children of God. Blessed are those who are persecuted for righteousness' sake, for theirs is the kingdom of heaven.

"Blessed are you when people revile you and persecute you and utter all kinds of evil against you falsely on my account. Rejoice and be glad, for your reward is great in heaven, for in the same way they persecuted the prophets who were before you."

The Sermon on the Mount is the heart of the gospel. It is here within this extended sermon that Jesus teaches us about prayer and about fasting, almsgiving, engaging in acts of mercy, and practicing forgiveness. Within the Sermon on the Mount we encounter the Beatitudes, which in a way is the heart of the Sermon on the Mount. The word *beatitude* means "blessing." The Beatitudes seem so simple, yet are so hard to follow: Blessed are the peacemakers, blessed are the meek, and blessed are those who mourn.

The Beatitudes are mileposts to the kingdom. Every time we find ourselves doing the things that Jesus expects of his faithful followers, we are getting one step closer to the kingdom. When driving on the interstate, I usually do not notice the mileposts on the side of the road, those small unassuming signs that tell us how far we are along the highway. While driving I tend to focus on the billboards on the side of the road or the large signs hanging from the overpass, and of course trying to pay attention to the cars in front and around me. Yet those mile markers are always there, informing me of how far I have traveled and how far I have to go toward my destination. The Beatitudes lead us one step closer to the kingdom, and even though we always don't have them in front of our mind, they are still there.

In the Beatitudes Jesus gives us concrete images for us to focus our attention on: peacemaking, being more meek and mild, comforting those that mourn, and so forth. However, when Jesus mentions the word *kingdom* I often have a vague notion of what he is telling me. Jesus refers to the kingdom as yeast. While yeast is so small and does nothing by itself, when added to water and flour it grows and grows into something wonderful. Likewise, Jesus refers to the kingdom as being like a mustard seed; again, something very small that gives birth to a large bush or tree. One of Jesus' sayings that I always remember is that the kingdom of God is within you. I often think, how can something so majestic, pure, and eternal be within me? Yet Jesus still reminds us that the kingdom of God is within us, within me and within you.

Jesus' teachings on the kingdom remind me of the classic C. S. Lewis series, the Chronicles of Narnia, especially the book *The Lion, the Witch, and the Wardrobe*. One day, while playing hide-and-seek, Lucy enters a large old-fashioned freestanding wardrobe. At first all she sees are old musty coats, but as she goes further into the large wardrobe, she enters into another world called Narnia, where, as Lewis says, it is always winter and never Christmas. Narnia has all the trappings of Christmas: the snow covering the trees and mountains, fire in the fire-place, hot tea and cookies. However, in Narnia, while it always looks like Christmas, but Christmas never comes. There is anticipation, but no fulfillment.

The story continues with Lucy and her siblings encountering talking beavers and bears, and creatures that are half-human and half-animal. Narnia seems like a world far, far away, off in a distant land and in a different place. Ironically, we find out that Narnia is not far away at all; it is just on the other side of the wardrobe. When Lucy enters the wardrobe, she walks through the coats and into Narnia.

Jesus reminds us that the kingdom of God is within us. It is already here. We might not always see it or even acknowledge it, but Jesus came to bring his Father's kingdom. All we have to do is open our hearts and our minds and we will see it. For me, Narnia is the perfect image of heaven, the final resolution of the good versus the bad. Aslan and his forces destroy the wicked White Witch. Afterward peace, mercy, and forgiveness reign. Isn't this what Jesus is talking about in the Beatitudes? If we follow them, we will enter into another world, a world where justice, peace, mercy, and forgiveness reign—a world where poverty and disease might not be finally destroyed but at least those who suffer will be comforted. Following the Beatitudes will lead us closer to Narnia, closer to the kingdom, but the good thing is that we don't have to travel too far!

Food for Thought

1. Take a few moments and reread the Beatitudes. Write down your thoughts and feelings about what Jesus is teaching us in these short but very powerful sayings.

2. The Word of God is not meant just to be studied and read, but to be lived out in our daily life. Take a few moments and reflect on how you can incorporate the Beatitudes in your life.

3. If you have time during this week, reread C. S. Lewis's *The Lion, The Witch, and the Wardrobe.* Especially read it in light of the gospel message of Jesus and the cross. What does this story tell us about the Christian message and faith? C. S. Lewis was a deeply committed Christian and his stories reveal much of the Christian faith in his writings.

4. For further reading: Isaiah 66:1–4; Luke 6:17–23; Romans 15:1–5

DAY 18

Tending the Vineyard
MARK 12:1–12

Then he began to speak to them in parables. "A man planted a vineyard, put a fence around it, dug a pit for the wine press, and built a watchtower; then he leased it to tenants and went to another country. When the season came, he sent a slave to the tenants to collect from them his share of the produce of the vineyard."

As Jesus was preaching and teaching, he used very common everyday images, metaphors, and symbols that people would easily understand. Jesus and his followers lived in an agrarian society that was based on farming, herding, and manual labor. Most of his followers were the poor, who worked the land and who intimately understood farming and agricultural images such as grape-growing as we see in Matthew.

However, Matthew was not the first one to use this image of the vineyard. This image goes way back, thousands of years ago, to the time of the prophet Isaiah. Isaiah begins his book with a wonderful story about a vineyard:

Let me sing for my beloved my love-song concerning his vineyard: My beloved had a vineyard on a very fertile hill. He dug it and cleared it of stones, and planted it with choice vines; he built a watchtower in the midst of it, and hewed out a wine vat in it.

Isaiah tells us that this is not any old vineyard, but the vineyard of the Lord. The Lord planted this vineyard in the land, and he cared for it so much that he built a fence around it to protect it from animals and from anything that would harm this vineyard. Then he put a watchtower in the middle of the vineyard so that the workers could climb up high on the watchtower to look for wild animals, which might harm the vineyard, or to look for approaching thunderstorms that might destroy the crops. Isaiah also tells us that the Lord dug a large vat and a wine press so that the red succulent grapes could be crushed for winemaking. In other words, Isaiah tells us that the Lord did everything he could to care for this tender young vineyard.

If we think that Isaiah's story is wonderful, we need to read further. Isaiah then tells us that instead of producing succulent, juicy red grapes, the vineyard produced wild grapes. Anyone who knows anything about growing grapes knows that wild vines do not produce grapes worth much. The Lord was so angry that his vineyard wasn't producing grapes that he removed the fence, destroyed the vat and the watchtower, and allowed first the weeds and then the neighbors to come and destroy the vineyard. Of course, Isaiah is not talking about growing grapes, but about Israel, God's chosen people.

However, the biblical God does not give up on his people. Even though they may wander off, worship other gods and idols, or worship in foreign temples, God still loves them very much and will go to extreme lengths to get Israel to return to them. One of the ancient images of the Church is a vineyard, as we hear in the common phrase "the Lord's vineyard." As members of this Church, we become servants of the Lord and workers in his vineyard. Through baptism in water and the Spirit, we are called to be good stewards of all that the Lord has entrusted to us. The land, the people, and all of our material possessions belong to him. We are merely caretakers of these things.

If you have ever visited a vineyard, you will know that the vines are not planted in one clump, but are planted in long straight rows. While walking through a vineyard, you see rows and rows of vines growing along wires and poles, which support these young vines. Likewise, it is quite impossible for one person to take care of the entire vineyard. Wineries employ hundreds of people to help plant the young vines, pick the ripe grapes, tend the vines, and do general work around the vineyard. The vines have to be pruned, fertilized, watered, and cared for. The grapes have to be pressed, bottled, fermented, and stored. Orders have to be taken and the wine has to be shipped. Vineyards employ many people to do all the work necessary to grow grapes. On average it takes between three and four years for a mature vine to produce juicy red grapes. Even after all of this hard work, you still do not know if you will make good wine from these grapes. So much can go wrong at various points in the winemaking process.

The Lord places both you and me in one row in the vineyard, along with other people. Our job is to take care of the tender sapling vines in that row. Our job is to do the weeding, feeding, and watering; tending to these young tender plants so that one day they will produce fruit. It really doesn't matter what is going on in the other rows in the vineyard—who is doing what, when, where, and how. So much of our time is wasted worrying about what other people are doing or not doing. This is not our concern. They will have to answer to the Lord for their work, just as we will have to answer to the Lord for our work.

The owner of the vineyard wants to see the results of our labor. He wants to see our fruit! One day we will have to give an account of what we have accomplished during our time planting, watering, feeding, and tending the vines in the vineyard. He will see if we were dedicated and devoted servants who worked diligently, or if we were slothful and lazy, because we were too busy keeping tabs on other people rather than working. If we are constantly scrutinizing the workers in the other rows of the vineyard and neglecting our own work, we will not be good servants. The Lord has invested a lot of time, energy, and work in planting this beautiful vineyard; hopefully we will be shown to be faithful servants!

Food for Thought

1. Where has the Lord planted you in his vineyard? What are some of the pains and joys in your life right now?

2. In Paul's Letter to the Galatians, he tells them to bear fruit of the Spirit (Gal 3). Take some time and make a list of the fruits of the Spirit. How can you cultivate these fruits in your life? In the life of your family? In your parish?

3. Christians are called to encourage one another, build one another up, and support one another. This week, try to make a conscientious effort to be a positive influence on someone in your congregation, family, or workplace.

4. For further reading: Matthew 10; Luke 16:12–16; 1 Corinthians 9:1–18; Ephesians 4:11–16

DAY 19

Who Is My Neighbor?
LUKE 10:25–37

Just then a lawyer stood up to test Jesus. "Teacher," he said, "what must I do to inherit eternal life?" He said to him, "What is written in the law? What do you read there?" He answered, "You shall love the Lord your God with all your heart, and with all your soul, and with all your strength, and with all your mind; and your neighbor as yourself." And he said to him, "You have given the right answer; do this, and you will live." But wanting to justify himself, he asked Jesus, "And who is my neighbor?"

Throughout the scriptures, the Pharisees and the Sadducees, the Jewish leaders, tried to trap Jesus in his own teaching. They constantly cited examples from the Old Testament to test whether or not Jesus would agree with their interpretation or not. They blamed Jesus for not following all of the religious rites and rituals, especially working on the Sabbath, which was a huge transgression at the time. When reading the gospels it seems as if the Jewish leaders were just waiting for Jesus to make a mistake so that they could get him in trouble.

Jesus' response to the man is based on the writing of the Old Testament, especially as found in the book of Deuteronomy, which is worth citing in full:

Hear, O Israel: The LORD is our God, the LORD alone. You shall love the LORD your God with all your heart, and with all your soul, and with all your might. Keep these words that I am commanding you today in your heart. Recite them to your children and talk about them when you are at home and when you are away, when you lie down and when you rise. Bind them as a sign on your hand, fix them as an emblem on your forehead, and write them on the doorposts of your house and on your gates. (Deut 6:4–9)

This passage is called the *Shema*, which is the Hebrew word that begins the phrase, "Hear O Israel." This passage is the heart of the scriptures since those who follow the Lord must obey this simple instruction of love—the love of God and the love of neighbor. Jesus even goes further and says that all the law and the prophets depends or rests on this one command of love. When we stop and think about it, this is a very important teaching since we often think of the numerous commandments and teachings of the prophets. Yet, Jesus summarizes all of this in one simple command of love.

Saying that I love someone is much easier than actually doing it! I often meet people whom I really don't care to be around, yet, I am again reminded of Jesus' words; the law of love is supreme. It is very difficult to love someone who verbally attacks you or who you know doesn't like you very much. There are so many people that are rough around the edges and may rub us the wrong way, yet the Lord has commanded us to love them.

Jesus says that a man was traveling from Jerusalem to Jericho and fell among robbers. This particular road was very important, it was a narrow and rocky road that was nearly 20 miles and went from 2500 feet above sea level to about 700 feet above sea level. Jericho was one of the popular cities in the Old Testament; it was in Jericho where Joshua blew his horn and the walls of the city came tumbling down. Jericho was also in the vicinities of the tribes of Benjamin and Joseph, two important tribes in the Old Testament. Furthermore, in the New Testament, Jericho is where Jesus heals Bartimaeus and later visits Zacchaeus who also lives in Jericho (Matt 20:29 and Luke 19:1).

The parable says that three different people walked by the man on the side of the road, a priest and a Levite, followed finally by a Samaritan. The priests and Levites were members of the religious elite in Judaism and hailed from the priestly lineage of Aaron. The Levites maintained the intricate rites, rituals, and ceremonies of the Temple. Luke does not tell us the exact reasons why both the priest and the Levite passed by the man alongside the road, but we can infer that, since the man was bloody, they refused to have contact with him. It was against the law to come into contact with anyone who was unclean or if there was blood involved. Or perhaps both the priest and Levite were late for a service in Jerusalem or had other errands to do and did not want to take the time to help someone.

Finally, a Samaritan came by and helped the injured man. This might not sound too impressive today, but during the time of Jesus, the Samaritans were considered religious and social outcasts. The Samaritans were a mixed race of Jews and pagans. They lived in the area called Samaria and were considered outcasts by the Jews. Samaritans are mentioned at several intervals in the scriptures; we have the famous story of Jesus and the Samaritan woman in the Gospel of John, who was living in adultery as mentioned in John 4. Thus, to the hearers of the gospel, this was a very strange thing, that an outsider stopped to help this man while the two Jewish priests, members of the children of Israel, did not help him.

The story also mentions that the Samaritan used his own material and financial resources to help the hurt man, using his own oil and wine to help cauterize the wounds and then put him on his beast and brought him to an inn. In the ancient world, oil and wine were used for food but also for medicinal purposes as well. Oil was a balm that helped soothe sores and wine was used as an antiseptic and it was used as a cleansing agent as we hear in the Book of Psalms: "and wine to gladden the human heart, oil to make the face shine, and bread to strengthen the human heart" (Ps 104:15). Many Christian Churches use oil in their sacramental rites for blessings and for healings; we have evidence of this in the Epistle of James, "Are any among you suffering? They should pray. Are any cheerful? They should sing songs of praise. Are any among you sick? They should call for the elders of the church and have them pray over them, anointing them with oil in the name of the Lord. The prayer of faith will save the sick, and the Lord will raise them up; and anyone who has committed sins will be forgiven" (Jas 5:13–15).

This parable is powerful as it shows us that love and compassion have no bounds. This Samaritan, a social outcast, took time out of his own day, at least an entire day, in order to assist with this beaten and hurt person. He also used his own money, which was at least two day's worth. We are reminded that we are called to do the same for other people as well. Jesus tells us that the entire law and the prophets can be reduced to one commandment — love of God and neighbor, "Hear, O Israel: the LORD our God is one LORD; and you shall love the LORD your God with all your heart, and with all your soul, and with all your might" (Deut 6:5). We fulfill one commandment by fulfilling the other, but both are needed. There is no limit to love just as there is no limit to forgiveness. At one point in the gospels, Jesus tells Peter that he is supposed to forgive seventy times seven, which is the biblical way of saying an infinite amount of times. Likewise, the love for the other is beyond limits. We should not distinguish between whom we should love or not. We should simply love! If we can do this one thing, perhaps we will have a chance to reach the heavenly kingdom.

Food for Thought

1. Take a few moments and write down a list of the immediate neighbors in your life. How

would you describe your relationship with them at this moment? Be as specific as possible. How can your relationship with your neighbors be improved?

2. Think of the many ways that you can express love for some of your neighbors. Sometimes small gestures go a long way, such as helping them shovel snow in the winter, cutting their grass in the summer, checking on them once in a while.

3. For further reading: Ruth 1—4; John 4:7–42; Acts 8:1–8

Day 20

Dying with Christ
GALATIANS 2:19–20

For through the law I died to the law, so that I might live to God. I have been crucified with Christ; and it is no longer I who live, but it is Christ who lives in me. And the life I now live in the flesh I live by faith in the Son of God, who loved me and gave himself for me. I do not nullify the grace of God; for if justification comes through the law, then Christ died for nothing.

Next to Jesus, the Apostle Paul is one of the most important people in Christianity. While working as a tentmaker, Paul traveled throughout the Roman Empire, preaching and teaching the kingdom of God, establishing new Christian communities, and correcting many divisions and debates in the Church. Paul was a bright, highly educated individual, a trained Pharisee who was well versed in the law and the prophets. He was trained under the famous Rabbi Gamaliel in Jerusalem and sailed across the Mediterranean with Barnabas, Silas, and Timothy. The central aspect of Paul's preaching is the cross of Christ, as we hear in the Letter to the Galatians, "It is not I who live but Christ who lives in me and who gave himself for me." The cross is God's sign of love for us.

Paul was like a son or daughter who comes home after school after earning an "A" on a report card or winning a soccer game or delivering a great performance in the school play. They're jumping up and down, screaming and shouting and acting so happy, wanting to tell you about their wonderful news. And what do you do? You listen for a while. But then your son or daughter goes on and on and on, talking a mile a minute, yapping away while you stand dumbfounded, and maybe even confused, trying to follow the incoherent conversation. After a while you say, "Okay already, okay, enough!"

Well, Paul was very much like that excited child. When he realized that Jesus was not just a miracle worker, or a prophet, or a teacher, but Jesus the Son of God, who was crucified on a gloomy Friday afternoon, Paul got so excited about this news that he started telling everyone about it! Everywhere Paul traveled, he shared this news about Jesus' death and resurrection. Paul traveled halfway across the world, by foot, by horse, and by ship, proclaiming to everyone God's love for the world.

Paul didn't wait for a council or a group of people to give him an invitation; he realized in his heart of hearts that this good news had to be shared with the rest of the world, and so he did. Paul conquered the world with the gospel of the cross, which was his weapon of peace. Just as the Romans conquered the world through power, coercion, fear, and force, Paul conquered the world through the love, peace, and forgiveness of the cross.

But why did Paul bother to do all of this in the first place? Paul could have easily stayed in his hometown of Tarsus, making tents and enjoying the easy life. When Paul was knocked off his horse on the way to Damascus, he realized that not only did his life change, but also that he was given the resources, gifts, and talents to preach this gospel. He used these gifts to build up the body of Christ, the Church. Just as Paul used his God-given gifts and talents to encourage and build up the Church, so too, are we supposed to use our God-given talents, abilities, resources, and experience to build up the body of Christ wherever we find ourselves—in our homes, in our parishes, and in our respective denominations. We are supposed to use all our God-given talents for Jesus' glory and not to sit on our backsides waiting for the Lord to come again.

Everyone has some God-given talents, resources, or abilities that can be used to build up and encourage one another. Each of us is born with a great big treasure chest full of talents to use, just like the ones that children play with when they play pirates and princesses. You know the ones with all of the bracelets, crowns, and jewels. But this treasure chest is different. This one is bottomless.

The more we look inside, the more we find. It keeps going and going. God has given each and every one of us a treasure chest full of wonderful talents to use to help one another.

We all have something to offer the world. Some of us have the ability to organize projects, others are financial wizards who are good with money, and others are good at teaching and sharing information. The Holy Spirit is the treasury of blessings and gifts. When Jesus died and rose from the dead, he sent the Holy Spirit into the world to complete the projects that he started. The Holy Spirit is alive and well in the Church today, even though we sometimes we don't always notice it!

Life is too short. Therefore, we have to be brutally honest with ourselves. Are we just sliding by in our spiritual life, living in survival mode like students who aim for a C because that is a passing grade, not striving for anything but the minimum? Sliding by is so common in our culture today, doing just enough, no more and no less. People just want to be average. Living average lives and having average jobs.

But does God want us merely to get by? Is that the message of the cross: just do the minimum? Did Paul just get by in life by doing the minimum? Did Jesus just get by in life doing the minimum? I don't think so. The message today is to for us to thrive and excel, using our God-given talents and abilities, even multiplying them, so that the preaching of the cross may be doubled in this world. Even tripled. Jesus' death on Golgotha wasn't cheap. It cost a lot in order for the gospel to be preached to the entire world. As the Lutheran pastor Dietrich Bonhoeffer said, there is no such thing as cheap grace. Jesus' death on the cross has given us a new lease on life. Are we going to sit back on our haunches and do nothing, or are we going to use our gifts for his glory and the glory of the kingdom?

Food for Thought

1. Many people think that they do not have any personal gifts or talents. This is simply not true. Everyone has something to offer humanity. Take a few moments and make an inventory of your talents and gifts. If you have a hard time doing this, ask a friend or a spouse to help you. Usually a friend or spouse will see things in your life that you might not always see.

2. Are you just getting by in life or are you thriving? Thriving means to excel and to use all of our energy and abilities that the Lord has given us. What is preventing you from thriving right now?

3. Talent is contagious. When a friend is doing well in school or work, very often you want to do well too. Make a conscious effort to share your recent accomplishments with your friends. Let them do the same with you. Maybe the both of you can grow together in the Lord.

4. For further reading: Jeremiah 1; Matthew 28; Romans 15

DAY 21

Locusts and Wild Honey
MARK 1:1–8

John the baptizer appeared in the wilderness, proclaiming a baptism of repentance for the forgiveness of sins. And people from the whole Judean countryside and all the people of Jerusalem were going out to him, and were baptized by him in the river Jordan, confessing their sins. Now John was clothed with camel's hair, with a leather belt around his waist, and he ate locusts and wild honey. He proclaimed, "The one who is more powerful than I is coming after me; I am not worthy to stoop down and untie the thong of his sandals. I have baptized you with water; but he will baptize you with the Holy Spirit."

Any parent worth their salt has heard, at least once, of the cute, huggable, orange-colored bear named Winnie the Pooh. Pooh eats wild honey and lives in the Hundred Acre Wood with Christopher Robin, Piglet, Eeyore, Tigger, and Owl. They have fun playing around, exploring caves and caverns, running and jumping over the hills and mountains. They fly kites and cajole, frolicking in the woods, enjoying a good adventure. And when things go wrong in the Hundred Acre Wood, which doesn't happen very often, they seem to work things out. If Tigger gets out of line, then Piglet talks to him. If Pooh gets lost, Christopher Robin goes and finds him. Each story usually ends with a happy ending. After all, isn't that comforting to children, that whatever the problem, at the end everyone seems to get along with one another.

There was a man who lived a long time ago who also ate locusts and wild honey, but he wasn't as cute and cuddly as Pooh. He didn't live in the lush, green Hundred Acre Wood with beautiful streams and budding flowers and lush grass. This man lived in the vast dry Judean wilderness. If you ever lived or visited the desert, it is hot, dry, and scary. Deserts are full of creepy-crawly insects, snakes, and other creatures. Deserts are scary places. This man's name was John.

John looked like a grizzly bear. He had long straggly hair and didn't bathe that much. He was very thin. John was a prophet because he came before Jesus in order to prepare his way. John was the sole voice in the desert wilderness, calling for repentance. In the scriptures, John is referred to as a "prophet" (Luke 7:26), "the baptist" (Matt 3:1), the "the greatest born of women" (Luke 7:28), and the "voice crying in the wilderness" (Mark 1:3). John is also known as the "forerunner" since he came before Jesus to prepare the way of repentance:

John was a "voice of one crying in the desert." As a prophet, John called people to repent and turn back to God. Isaiah told the Israelites to stop worshipping false gods and turn to the one true living God, the God of Abraham, Isaac, and Jacob. However, the Israelites, like us, preferred to worship false gods and idols, "Their land is filled with idols; they bow down to the work of their hands, to what their own fingers have made" (Isa 2:8). John appeared as a voice in the wilderness, as another Isaiah, ultimately to prepare the way for Jesus. However,

John, like most of the prophets, was persecuted for his preaching.

John the Baptist lived all alone in that desert; he didn't have many friends like Pooh and Piglet, Eeyore or Tigger. And one day out of the blue, John started to preach the gospel in the middle of that wilderness; he preached that God's kingdom was coming. People in the surrounding areas heard about this crazy guy who was living in the desert so they went out to see him. And what were his first words to them? He didn't say, "Hey, nice weather we're having!" or "How are you doing?" The first words out of his mouth were, "You brood of vipers, repent for the kingdom of God is at hand. Repent for the Lord is coming. Repent for God's son has arrived." Of all the names that John could have called them, he called them vipers, not a term of endearment in my book. A viper is a very deadly snake that slithers and slides across the desert land. Vipers are very deadly; they can kill a man with one bite. John calls them vipers, which means not just one snake, but a lot of them! Yet people kept on going out to see John in the desert and they were baptized.

However, a lot of people looked around and thought to themselves, "Why should I change when life is good?" The Sea of Galilee was bountiful, and many families were making a good living catching fish. Despite real political discontent in Judea at the time, the *Pax Romana* made it possible for people to live their lives without worrying about wars or invasions. There was plenty of money to be made, and merchants were happy. People in Jerusalem were more or less content with their lifestyles. But when John looked around, what did *he* see? He saw that, yes, there were jobs, happy families, and economic prosperity for many. But he also saw that there were poor people hanging around the Temple in Jerusalem with no one to help them. He saw widows and orphans whose husbands and fathers had been arrested and executed for political reasons. He saw the homeless and the hopeless with no one to take care of them. He saw that no one cared.

John wasn't so unique. His message was the same message of all the prophets and the same message of Jesus: Repent for the kingdom of God has come. John told them and us that life is now different because God's son has arrived. Look around, and change your life. Look around and get with the program.

Not much has changed in two thousand years. There is still poverty, homelessness, hunger, and war. Why, in our country, which is one of the richest countries in the world, do we have poor people living under bridges and under buildings? Why are there still homeless shelters and soup kitchens? Why are there pregnant women with nowhere to go? Sure, the government will always try to intervene, but they can never keep up with the need. It's up to us to care for them. The poor and needy depend on us for their daily bread. The pregnant teens with nowhere to go need us for care and comfort. Those unlovable people need us to love them. They depend on us for comfort. They depend on us for hope. That is why people flocked to Jesus and John because they saw John and Jesus as their only hope. They heard the gospel and found comfort.

Food for Thought

1. Identify a few of the major social needs in your neighborhood or community. What ways can your parish get more involved in community action?

2. John the Baptist was one of the last great prophets. The prophets were powerful preachers. Take some time this week and read some of the prophets. You might want to start with one of the shorter ones, such as Amos, Hosea, Jonah, or Micah. Once you get comfortable reading them, turn to the longer ones such as Isaiah, Jeremiah, or Ezekiel. When I am down or distressed, I turn to the prophets for hope and encouragement. I hope you will too!

3. John the Baptist, like Jesus, was not well liked by the Jewish leaders. Great prophets are not usually accepted by their communities. However, the prophets are very powerful, heralding in winds of change. We have been blessed to have so many prophets in our time: Malcolm X, Martin Luther King Jr, Mother Teresa, Dorothy Day, Pope John Paul II, Oscar Romero, and Dietrich Bonhoeffer, among others.

4. For further reading: Ezekiel 3; Luke 4:16–27; Hebrews 10

Day 22

Become Like Children
Matthew 18:1–5

At that time the disciples came to Jesus and asked, "Who is the greatest in the kingdom of heaven?" He called a child, whom he put among them, and said, "Truly I tell you, unless you change and become like children, you will never enter the kingdom of heaven. Whoever becomes humble like this child is the greatest in the kingdom of heaven. Whoever welcomes one such child in my name welcomes me."

The New Testament contains four Gospels: Matthew, Mark, Luke, and John. These are not meant to be read as biographies in the modern sense, like biographies of Winston Churchill, Jimmy Carter, or Billy Graham. Nor are they like modern histories of North America, Europe, or Asia. The gospels are stories of faith. Each gospel contains the entire truth about Jesus the Son of God, but in slightly different ways. For example, suppose you witness a car accident on the way to work. You stop in order to see if anyone needs help. A police car pulls up and the officer wants to know how the accident took place. You and another witness tell the officer your story. The versions are slightly different, but the one thing that the both of you have in common is that you both saw the car accident. The police officer will need to have many witnesses in order to ascertain what led to the accident. Each person may recount slightly different versions of the accident, depending on their particular vantage point. This same situation pertains to the gospel. Matthew, Mark, Luke, and John provide us with four witnesses to the preaching, teaching, and miracles of Jesus Christ. Likewise, the four Gospels contain various teachings, sermons, and healings, yet they all emphasize one important fact: our discipleship in Jesus' name.

The disciples in the gospel reading did not understand this. Perhaps they thought that they could buy their way, not only into the kingdom, but into being the greatest in the kingdom, like someone could slip the maître d' a twenty-dollar bill to get a good seat in a restaurant. Matthew tells us that Jesus doesn't work this way. You cannot buy your way into the kingdom. Following Jesus does not require money, power, prestige, name-dropping, networking, or titles. The only thing that Jesus wants is for us to be totally and completely dependent on him. We cannot follow Jesus if we are full of our self.

Yet we know this is contrary to the ways of the world. A common phrase is "money talks," which means that money opens doors. We always hear of wealthy moguls who donate large sums of money to their alma mater so that their sons or daughters can get into a prestigious prep school or university. Or how many contractors or developers try to influence the voting records of local government officials so that their development plans will pass the zoning board? In our culture, money is equated with power, prestige, and profit.

However, we know that Jesus works in a slightly different manner. Power, profit, and prestige may be the way of the world, but it is not the way of Jesus. Jesus wants us to be dependent on him, as children are dependent on their parents. This is a bit ironic since we know that Jesus himself was not married nor had children of his own, yet he uses the example of children in order to teach his followers what it means to be his disciple. The passage is paraphrased in the following way: Unless you turn and become like a child you will never enter in the kingdom of Heaven. The next passage is that, if you prevent one of these children from coming to me, it would be better if a millstone were tied around your neck and you were cast into the sea.

Children are totally dependant on their parents or caregivers. They cannot feed themselves so their parents feed them. Toddlers cannot get dressed or go to school by themselves so parents have to clothe them and drive them to school. Parents have to help them with their homework. In other words, children are utterly dependant on the love and care of other people to help them learn what it means to be a human person. Matthew tells us that this is what Jesus demands from his followers, utter dependence on God for our sustenance, for our food, and for everything that we need to get through this life.

However, the second saying about children is a very hard statement. Jesus tells us that if we prevent other children from coming to him, from following and listening to his teaching, then it would be better if we were thrown into the sea with a millstone around our neck. Millstones are very large stones that are turned by either a donkey or a water wheel and are used to grind wheat into flour or corn into cornmeal. They are extremely heavy and cannot be moved easily. I don't know about you, but I certainly don't want a millstone tied around my neck anytime soon!

There are similar warnings in the gospel that basically teach the same message. Jesus tells his disciples that the last shall be first and the first shall be last, that he who humbles himself will be exalted and he who exalts himself will be humbled, that even if you say "Lord, Lord," you will not enter the kingdom. These warnings are for us that we need to take our faith seriously. Why put off tomorrow what we should be doing today? We all are born with an expiration date; no one lives forever. We will die someday and eternity is a long, long, very long time! Why do we want to take the chance and be shut out of the kingdom? I certainly don't want to be on the outside of those pearly gates, looking in at a great dinner party. Maybe we can take Jesus' message as a warning now so that we won't be found in a lurch later on in life.

Food for Thought

1. Our culture teaches us that we are supposed to be self-reliant. Others say that the go-getters are the ones who pull their own bootstraps up and get ahead in this world. We are supposed to use the gifts that the Lord has given us; at the same time, we need to thank him for these gifts.

2. Children spend so much time exploring the world around them. They lead very simple lives, searching out the mystery hidden in all living creatures. They get joy out of small things

in life, an ice cream cone, watching a bird fly, smelling flowers, and taking a walk in the park. Have you tried to simplify your life lately?

3. For further reading: Mark 9:33–37; Luke 9:46–48

Day 23

Gardening with God
1 Corinthians 3:5–8

What then is Apollos? What is Paul? Servants through whom you came to believe, as the Lord assigned to each. I planted, Apollos watered, but God gave the growth. So neither the one who plants nor the one who waters is anything, but only God who gives the growth. The one who plants and the one who waters have a common purpose, and each will receive wages according to the labor of each.

Imagine that your family is vacationing at the beach in the summertime. The hot sun warms your skin as you watch the blue ocean waves gently roll along the sand. Groups of pelicans fly overhead. A girl is flying a kite with her daddy. People sunbathe. A mom sits in a lounge chair reading a book. A young boy is frolicking in the surf. Your son or daughter wants you to help build a sand castle. So of course, being a good parent, you say yes, and the two of you begin work.

At first you think that it will be a small sand castle, but your son has other plans—he wants an entire village complete with castle, moat, and walls! You spend hours building this castle, walking across the beach with your beach bucket collecting sand. You begin constructing your sand castle carefully by piling on the sand one bucket at a time. After a while the two of you decide to stop and have lunch, so you walk back to your blanket across the beach and have lunch while enjoying your time together as a family. After eating your sandwiches and drinks, you walk back to the sand castle and, lo and behold! What do you see? Your sand castle is damaged. Not only damaged but totally destroyed. The tall towers that you worked so hard on are now flattened and the moat that went around the castle is filled with water. The entire castle has quickly turned to just a pile of sand.

How would you react to this situation? Would you be happy, shouting, "Hurray, my sand castle is destroyed!" or would you be indifferent saying, "Oh well, my sand castle is destroyed," or perhaps you would you be angry, upset, flabbergasted that your wonderful sand castle that took you two whole hours to build was messed up! I am almost positive that most of us would be very, very angry.

Paul was upset, too, when he found out that his newly planted mission in Corinth was slowly falling apart. Corinth is a city in Greece that has two major ports for shipping, and the land is connected by an isthmus, a small land-bridge. Paul was like a master gardener, sowing seeds in his new mission field in Corinth. The Book of Acts tells us that he was there for at least a year-and-a-half, preaching and leading the congregations. This was all great work. Paul was proud of his accomplishments. Paul traveled throughout the Roman Empire sowing seeds of the gospel.

Then Paul left the area so that he could sow seeds in other places. Behind Paul's back, his so-called friends, and I use this term loosely, entered his mission field, and basically said, "Ah, you don't have to believe what Paul told you. He's not really a teacher anyway; he's a bit crazy. We'll tell you what you have to know." So these so-called friends came and messed up Paul's beautiful garden; they planted weeds of division and doubt. These bad weeds grew up with the good seeds that Paul planted. And Paul got so angry because these weeds were growing and growing and growing and were taking over these small seedlings. It was like wild kudzu taking over his communities. So Paul wrote a strong letter telling them to return to his teaching so that they could grow and survive. Paul had to rip out the weeds that were overtaking the garden in Corinth.

Well, perhaps you didn't know it, but even though Paul is long gone, he still plants seeds. Every time we open the Bible and read his letters or hear them in a sermon, we are receiving a little seed of the kingdom. Week after week, season after season, Paul sows his seeds in our hearts. He plants these seeds and hopefully they will grow. We are usually pretty happy about this; most people enjoy being in a church with one another, and having another seed planted in us.

Jesus says that a sower went out and sowed his seeds. Some fell along the path and were trampled underfoot. Some fell on the rock and after it grew a little bit, it withered away due to lack of water. Some fell along the thorns, which choked the seed. Finally some fell in the good soil and it yielded a large harvest, Luke says hundredfold.

According to Jesus, the seed is the Word of God that is planted. The sower continues to sow his seeds no matter where they may fall on the earth. In other words, the sower does not have control over where the seeds will fall nor does he have control whether or not the seeds will grow. His job is only to sow, as we see in Paul's First Letter to the Corinthians:

> *I planted, Apollos watered, but God gave the growth. So neither the one who plants nor the one who waters is anything, but only God who gives the growth. The one who plants and the one who waters have a common purpose, and each will receive wages according to the labor of each. For we are God's servants, working together; you are God's field, God's building. (1 Cor 3:6–9)*

Paul was the first one to preach the gospel to the Corinthians. Apollos followed Paul in his teaching and was the one who Paul says watered, but ultimately God gave the growth of the gospel as the Corinthian community continued to grow and increase. Paul had no control over the expansion of his communities; the growth of the gospel depended solely on God alone.

The hope is that the seed, which is really the Word of God, finds the good soil and takes root, grows, and provides an abundant harvest. The good soil is described of being a good and honest heart that accepts the Word and allows it to flourish. In the scriptures the word *heart* is the very core or center of a person, the life force that keeps the body going. The head or brain was considered the rational or thinking aspect of a person, but the heart was the center. Thus, if the heart was good and honest then the person could hear the gospel and it would grow. If the heart was not honest, truthful, and open, the gospel would not grow.

However, the goal of sowing seeds is not just to sow the seed but hopefully to reap a large harvest. No one plants a garden and expects just a few vegetables and flowers. When planting a garden we usually look forward to a huge crop of tomatoes, peppers, and cucumbers. No one plants a garden just to look at the nice green leaves. It is one thing to plant a garden, but if a tomato plant does not bring forth tomatoes, then what good is the plant? If my apple tree does not bring forth apples, what good is the apple tree? In other words, the hope is that the seeds produce fruit, and Luke states that it will produce a hundredfold.

The garden imagery that Jesus uses is a good one. When starting a garden we have to prepare the soil, remove all the weeds, rocks, stones, and leaves that fell on the ground and accumulated during the autumn and winter months. Then we have to dig the soil and bring humus and other dead material in so that the soil will be good. We may bring some fertilizer to help the plants grow. Then we actually purchase the plants and seeds and plant the garden. Planting a garden is very hard work and anyone who has done that knows the difficulty involved. However, we cannot have a good harvest if we do not take the time to prepare the soil and get everything ready.

The Church offers us various ways to help us prepare the "soil" of our heart: praying and fasting, participating in the sacrament of confession and holy communion, reading and reflecting on the lives of the saints, and regularly reading and studying the scriptures. These various activities are not ends in themselves but are ways in which we prepare our heart to hear the Word and that it can blossom and bear fruits of repentance.

Food for Thought

1. Hearing the Word of God is not always easy. Sometimes we miss the message. Make a list of some spiritual practices that might help you better hear the Word of God. These practices are not foolproof, but are ways that people in the past have tried to create a soft heart to hear the gospel.

2. When you attend Sunday services, do you always remember the sermon that was preached? Most people hear the sermon on Sunday and then by Monday morning they have already forgotten it. Don't worry, there are techniques to help you remember. After church, take time while driving home and discuss the sermon in the car with your family. On Sunday night, before going to bed, think of the main point of the sermon. Use this main point as a way to keep that seed firmly planted in your heart during the week. Think about the sermon on Tuesday, Wednesday, and Thursday. You

will be surprised how this small seed begins to grow.

3. For further reading: Jeremiah 32:36–41; Acts 9:1–22

DAY 24

The Poor You Shall Always Have with You
LUKE 16:19–23

There was a rich man who was dressed in purple and fine linen and who feasted sumptuously every day. And at his gate lay a poor man named Lazarus, covered with sores, who longed to satisfy his hunger with what fell from the rich man's table; even the dogs would come and lick his sores. The poor man died and was carried away by the angels to be with Abraham. The rich man also died and was buried. In Hades, where he was being tormented, he looked up and saw Abraham far away with Lazarus by his side.

Recently I had the joy of visiting my brother-in-law in Chicago. Chicago is a very beautiful city, full of beautiful sights and sounds, and the home of some great architecture. It is also a very windy city and cold in the wintertime. It is the home of the famous Willis (formerly Sears) Tower, and of course, the Bulls, Bears, White Sox, and Cubs.

However, Chicago also has a darker side to it. Like other large cities, among the hustle and bustle and wonderful art and architecture, the city has a lot of poverty. While walking down the many streets one encounters panhandlers begging for money, homeless men and women. I vividly remember one woman sitting in a wheelchair who was an amputee. She had no legs and couldn't walk. Others were lying on the ground and some were sleeping under the trees in Millennium Park. What a strange sight, lining the streets of what Chicagoans call the "Gold Coast" were many of the homeless, the poor, the lame, and the blind.

It is easy to judge the poor. Some are clearly addicted to alcohol and others to drugs. Their stumbling gaits and bad breath, their incoherent speech, reveal hardscrabble lives. Others are pregnant and probably not married. Others are probably irresponsible and couldn't hold down a job. It is easy to look down at the poor, blaming their current plight as their having made poor choices in life. People often ask: Why should I help them? Our tax money goes for public assistance, low cost housing, free butter and cheese, and many shelters around the city. These are the Lazaruses of the world, roaming the streets, asking for handouts, seeking the crumbs from our table.

Luke tells us about an unnamed rich man who was living lavishly in his large house while a poor man named Lazarus was begging outside his gates. It is interesting that Luke does not name the rich man while the poor man was named; it makes the poor man more human, more personal, while the rich man seems very impersonal. We must keep in mind that this Lazarus is not the same

Lazarus that we hear about in the Gospel of John. The name Lazarus is derived from the Hebrew word *Eleazar*, which means, "God has helped." We will see later in the story how God has helped the poor Lazarus.

The plot thickens as we hear of dogs licking Lazarus's wounds. In antiquity, dogs were dirty animals and Luke says that these dirty and unclean animals actually took better care of Lazarus than did the rich man. The story takes a turn when both men die and Lazarus finds himself in heaven, or, as Luke says, in Abraham's bosom. However, the rich man was in torments in Hades, which is the realm of the dead. In the Old Testament Hades is also referred to as Sheol, which is the place of death and darkness. If people were in Hades, it meant that they were dead and could no longer offer their praise and prayer to God.

The rich man begs Abraham to send Lazarus to soothe his anguish, yet Abraham refuses to fulfill his request. There is a great chasm or gulf between heaven and Hades. Then the rich man asks if Abraham would send Lazarus to his five brothers as a warning. Again, Abraham says no. They have Moses and the prophets, and if they cannot believe what is written there, they will never believe a miracle of someone coming back from the dead (Luke 16:31). This may seem like a harsh saying. One would think that the rich man is generally concerned about the welfare and future of his brothers. By sending Lazarus, he thinks that this will increase his brothers' faith and commitment to the Lord and will change their ways. However, Jesus himself says that if people cannot believe Moses and the things that are written about the messiah, they will certainly not listen to him either: "If you believed Moses, you would believe me, for he wrote about me. But if you do not believe what he wrote, how will you believe what I say?" (John 5:45–47).

People generally seek signs or miracles to increase their faith. Yet Luke is telling us something very important. The scriptures are the basis for our faith. Miracles may occur now and then but our faith is not in the miracle, but in the teaching of the gospel. The Apostle Paul reminds us that even a demon can come disguised as an angel of light. A second important lesson in this parable is that the love of God is intimately connected with the love of the neighbor. Throughout the scriptures God commands his people to love the poor, the orphan, and the widow because it is when we love our neighbor that we learn to love God:

> "When the Son of Man comes in his glory, and all the angels with him, then he will sit on the throne of his glory. All the nations will be gathered before him, and he will separate people one from another as a shepherd separates the sheep from the goats, and he will put the sheep at his right hand and the goats at the left. Then the king will say to those at his right hand, 'Come, you that are blessed by my Father, inherit the kingdom prepared for you from the foundation of the world; for I was hungry and you gave me food, I was thirsty and you gave me something to drink, I was a stranger and you welcomed me, I was naked and you gave me clothing, I was sick and you took care of me, I was in prison and you visited me.' " (Matt 25:31–36)

As Christians we are called not just to hear and learn the gospel but also to do it. The poor Lazarus was sitting by this man's gate day after day and the rich man chose not to see the reality that there was a poor and needy person who was literally at his feet begging for food. Yet the rich man chose not to help him. In the end it was too late since he was given an entire lifetime to perform acts of charity and love. We might think that Abraham's response to the rich man is rather cold, that he refuses to send Lazarus to his brothers or even to cool the tip of his tongue. Yet we know that there are some people who will not believe even if they experience a great miracle! Luke's message is that we are called to love both God and neighbor now; if we put it off until tomorrow it will be too late.

From the vantage point of the gospel, we are like the rich man in the gospel, feasting sumptuously, wearing robes of purple, living in luxury among those who are less fortunate than we. We may not drive Bentleys or BMWs or have two homes, but we are certainly rich in so many other ways. We feast on the Word of God. We feast on the Eucharist. We feast on the sheer beauty of creation. Surely we can share our crumbs with those who are less fortunate; with the hungry, the homeless, the poor, the naked, the sick, and the suffering; with those who are hungry and thirsty for hope and peace in this world; with those who are imprisoned by their own demons.

But there is another kind of poverty too. While strolling the streets of Chicago, I also encountered many tourists and businessmen and women who were hurrying along at a very brisk pace. When I was young my mother once told me that people's "eyes don't lie" and that the "eyes are the window into a person's soul." I looked into a lot of hollow and empty eyes, eyes that stared into nowhere, with no life in them. Perhaps some of them had a bad marriage or were hungry for compassion. Others might have been depressed or fallen into despair. Others perhaps had a deep sense of emptiness or loss, or were hungry for love and direction in life. These also are the poor, the hungry, and the homeless of the world. Maybe today we can share our riches with those who don't have any. We might even feel good helping a fellow pilgrim.

Food for Thought

1. We often think of poverty merely in terms of financial or material goods. However, people can also be spiritually poor. Make a list of those around you who you think are suffering from spiritual poverty. Perhaps they have no friends, maybe they are mourning the loss of a loved one, or maybe they lost a job. How can you better help those in your life who are suffering spiritually? How can your parish community better help people in need?

2. What are some of the things that you have done recently to make someone else's life easier? How have you helped a friend or neighbor? How did it make you feel after you were done?

3. For further reading: Ezekiel 34; Acts 6; James 2

DAY 25

Looking for God in All the Wrong Places
MARK 5:1–20

They came to the other side of the lake, to the country of the Gerasenes. And when he had stepped out of the boat, immediately a man out of the tombs with an unclean spirit met him. He lived among the tombs; and no one could restrain him any more, even with a chain; for he had often been restrained with shackles and chains, but the chains he wrenched apart, and the shackles he broke in pieces; and no one had the strength to subdue him. Night and day among the tombs and on the mountains he was always howling and bruising himself with stones. When he saw Jesus from a distance, he ran and bowed down before him; and he shouted at the top of his voice, "What have you to do with me, Jesus, Son of the Most High God?"

Over the years people often ask me why we do not experience miracles like people did back in the time of Jesus. Once in a while people might have a near-death experience and they see Jesus basking in a white light standing at the end of a tunnel. Others may have a vision of the Virgin Mary or Saint Francis or an image of a departed mother, father, or friend.

The Bible is full of miracles: Moses parting the Red Sea, Elijah healing the widow's son, Jesus driving out demons. Of course, there are what I call the "big" miracles: Paul's conversion and, of course, Jesus' resurrection from the dead. These don't happen very often.

Today, when people experience a miracle they often chalk it up to good science, medicine, or merely a coincidence, a random act of nature. Take, for example, the horror of the 9/11 terrorist attacks. At 9:00 a.m. on the morning of 9/11 workers left their offices in the Twin Towers to get coffee and bagels for coworkers; a common practice in most parts of New York City. Ten minutes later two jet airplanes flew right into the towers, killing thousands of people and maiming hundreds more. Many survivors considered their absence from these buildings a miracle. Other people say that it was a purely coincidental event since coffee runs are commonplace in big companies.

Not too far from where we live, a small private jet plane fell out of the sky. Thankfully no one was hurt, not even the pilot, who was found intact, sitting in the cockpit, which was perched atop a tree. Experts reported that the pilot's survival was due to wind sheer, which allowed the plane to fall in a certain way, gracefully falling into a large oak tree, safe and sound. Yet the newspapers say that his survival was "miraculous."

Perhaps these events or situations are a gift to us from God, giving us a glimpse of the kingdom of heaven. After all, this is what miracles are anyway, little glimpses into God's power and authority, even over nature. If he created the world in six days and pushed back the waters of the Nile to allow Israel to cross over, he can surely allow pilots to escape unharmed and women to survive difficult births. Yet, just like the people in the gospels, we miss the true meaning of the miracle.

Not much as changed since Biblical times, as the author of the Book of Ecclesiastes says: "There is nothing new under the sun." Then, as now, people want to be entertained. They want to be razzle-dazzled with the "ooh" and the "ahhh" of Jesus. During Jesus' time there were magicians, fortune-tellers, and astrologers. Yet, Jesus was not a magician nor was he trying to entertain people, although many thought they were being entertained. At one point, when Jesus multiplied the loaves and fishes, they wanted to seize him in order to make him a king! They saw his power in human terms, missing the point that Jesus was directing them to the kingdom. Jesus' miracles are a sign of his kingship, but his kingship is not of this world. His power is over disease, nature, and even death. God is God over all things in creation. These miracles, like Jesus driving out demons, are an invitation of faith.

The gospels include many of Jesus' miracles of healing: the woman who had a flow of blood, the Roman centurion's servant who was ill, and the cleansing of the lepers. These people approached Jesus in faith, and they were healed of their disease and discomfort because of their faith; because they came to Jesus for help. And compared to the "big" miracles that we often think about, the parting of the Red Sea for instance, these miracles in the gospel are quite small. Jesus really didn't do much. He says a few words and people are restored to health and well-being.

Yet all too often we overlook the hundreds of small miracles in our life, the small glimpses into the kingdom of God, because we are too darn busy seeking the big miracles, the walking-on-water type or the resurrection.

We overlook the many miracles of family members being reconciled to their family after being pushed out or living in self-induced exile, the miracle of a restored friendship, and the miracle of life itself. I think we do this because deep down we would rather be entertained and excited and we don't want Jesus interfering in our life. After all, it is a fearful thing when we encounter the Lord. The great crowds of the Gerasenes were afraid because of what Jesus did to the possessed man; they were so afraid that they demanded that Jesus leave them immediately. Often we push Jesus out of our life too because we can't deal with the kingdom. We want to focus on the here and now. How sad, because all the while Jesus was directing these people to the kingdom, offering them the bread of life, and they were satisfied with popcorn and cotton candy. How sad, indeed!

Food for Thought

1. The sacrament of confession and reconciliation is a great way to drive out our hidden demons that we carry around with us. Have you participated in confession recently? You may find that confessing all of your sins to a priest will make you feel better and clear your conscience.

2. Very often events in our life appear to be larger than life and overwhelming. Where does evil manifest itself in your family, with your friends, at your work, or in your parish? How can you fight this evil and change it into good?

3. For further reading: Matthew 8:28–34; Ephesians 6:10–18; Peter 2:1–12

Day 26

Waiting for Jesus
Matthew 1:1–17

An account of the genealogy of Jesus the Messiah, the son of David, the son of Abraham. Abraham was the father of Isaac, and Isaac the father of Jacob, and Jacob the father of Judah and his brothers, and Judah the father of Perez and Zerah by Tamar, and Perez the father of Hezron, and Hezron the father of Aram, and Aram the father of Aminadab, and Aminadab the father of Nahshon, and Nahshon the father of Salmon, and Salmon the father of Boaz by Rahab, and Boaz the father of Obed by Ruth, and Obed the father of Jesse, and Jesse the father of King David.

If I am on the road traveling, I will sometimes stop at the local Starbucks for a cup of coffee. Usually I just go right in and order and then leave. Sometimes if I am in a hurry, I will go through the drive-through window if there is one. During the Christmas season everything gets extra crowded, even the local Starbucks. One year while I was doing some last-minute Christmas shopping, I really wanted to have a hot cup of coffee, so I walked into the local Starbucks. I was almost drooling thinking about sipping a tall Grande coffee of the day and a chocolate chunk brownie to go with it. I was in a hurry so I wanted to be in and out of the store very quickly. Not this time! I usually don't mind long lines, but this time it was ridiculous. Grandparents, parents, and children, girls with their boyfriends, were in line ahead of me. The line snaked through the store right to the front entrance. I never saw so many people waiting for coffee! So I waited too. I was cold and thirsty, and needed a little caffeine pick-me-up to get through the end of a long day Christmas shopping. At this point I would wait an extra thirty minutes if I had to.

We spend too much time each and every day waiting for things. Have you ever noticed that so much of your life is spent waiting at stoplights? Let's say we have to go through four intersections in order to get to work and each stoplight is about three minutes long. That means if we time it wrong and have to stop at four red lights going to and from work each way, that is about twenty-four minutes of our day wasted. There are so many other things that we could be doing with our time than wait at a red light.

Sometimes waiting can be mentally excruciating. There is nothing worse than going for a checkup and then waiting for the results of a medical test. After going to the doctor's office and getting the test, you assume that you will know the results at the end of the day. But the doctor tells you that you'll have to wait. It is only Thursday afternoon. You are notified that you have to wait until Monday when the results will be back. The doctor will call you on Tuesday. You have to wait through a long weekend. You might feel fine but your mind begins to wonder and think about all the terrible and awful diseases that are around, the flu, tuberculosis, even pneumonia! You wait and wait and wait until Monday for the results.

Or perhaps you are stuck in a very bad job. You go to work and punch the clock but you are not happy. So you apply for some better-paying jobs that you might be good at doing. After applying they tell you, "Don't call us, we'll call you." This type of waiting is bad. You wait by the phone anxiously waiting it to ring, thinking it might be the job of a lifetime. But that call never comes. You wait some more, applying for other jobs.

A good friend of mine once told me that probably 95 percent of our day is spent in waiting. We wait for oil changes, haircut appointments; we wait in line for coffee and at the bank. We are constantly in waiting mode. And isn't this what the season of Advent is, a time of waiting? We aren't waiting for coffee or an oil change; we are waiting for the coming of the Lord, for Jesus to be born.

Advent is a special season to prepare us for Jesus' birth. In the Western Church calendar it lasts for four consecutive Sundays. In the Eastern Church Calendar it lasts for forty days. During this time we encounter special hymns, such as "O Come, O Come, Immanuel" and special prayers. We patiently await the manger and Joseph and Mary and the visitation of the shepherds, and, of course, the visitation of the wise men, bringing their gifts of gold, frankincense, and myrrh. Many parishes host special music concerts and recitals; others put on Christmas plays and tableaus for the public. And of course there is the required live Nativity scene complete with live animals and hot chocolate and fresh apple cider.

The Bible tells us that God's people had to wait a long time for Jesus' birth. They waited centuries, even millennia. Matthew begins his Gospel with a very long list of names; some of them sound so strange to us today. These are the ancestors of Jesus who waited a very long time to see him. Some were kings, others were fearless warriors, others were patriarchs and leaders.

At one point some Israelites thought that maybe King David was the messiah, the savior, but he wasn't. He was somewhat of a good king, a strong leader uniting the tribes of Israel. He didn't fit the job description. Later in the times of the New Testament some Jews thought John the Baptist was the one but he was only Jesus' cousin. He certainly had his good qualities; he was a great preacher spending a lot of time in the wilderness. But he himself said that he wasn't the Christ. No, the Christ was to be born in Bethlehem, a small village in Judea. His mother was Mary. Joseph was going to take care of them, first taking them on their first family "vacation" to Egypt in order to escape the jealous King Herod, and then back to Nazareth where they settled down and opened a carpenter's shop.

We wait in expectation, searching, hoping, and yearning for the light of the world to be born, the light that shines in the darkness, the light of the Gentiles. It is this newborn babe, wrapped in swaddling clothes, this young child who would conquer the world, not with the sword, but with a word, a word of hope and joy; a word of forgiveness and mercy; word of comfort and consolation. This is whom we are waiting for this Advent.

This period of Advent also involves many practical tasks that have to be completed: baking, shopping, wrapping presents, sending cards, more baking, and then of course decorating the house with the tree, wreaths, and all the trimmings. Not to mention the large Christmas dinner that you promised to cook! These tasks get piled on higher and higher. You might even feel overwhelmed at times; I know I do.

During this time of the Christmas hustle and bustle, perhaps we can spend some quiet time in reflection on *the reason for the season*. The trees and the trimmings and the cookies and the carols are wonderful. Our family always watches the local live Nativity scene; my daughters are fixated on Mary and her little baby. I love coming home and smelling fresh bread baking in the oven or the outdoor smell of a newly cut Frazier fir. However, all this preparation comes short if we forget that the "reason for the season" is the babe born in Bethlehem, Christ the Lord.

Food for Thought

1. Advent is a period of patient waiting. During the Advent season, feel free to take time each week and reflect on Old Testament prophecies about the coming of Christ. You can even read these stories together as a family, which will make your Christmas even more meaningful.

2. The period between Thanksgiving and Christmas is known as shopping season for gifts, trinkets, and all types of things for family, neighbors, or coworkers. This year, in order to

make this Christmas a little extra special, maybe you and your family can decide to adopt a local charity or food pantry. I am sure they would gladly appreciate your generosity. If you are not aware of a local charity you can contact a local church. Usually they can be of some assistance.

3. For further reading: Isaiah 9; Micah 7:14–20; Luke 3:23–38

DAY 27

Walking with the Lord
EPHESIANS 5:15–19

Be careful then how you live, not as unwise people but as wise, making the most of the time, because the days are evil. So do not be foolish, but understand what the will of the Lord is. Do not get drunk with wine, for that is debauchery; but be filled with the Spirit, as you sing psalms and hymns and spiritual songs among yourselves, singing and making melody to the Lord in your hearts, giving thanks to God the Father at all times and for everything in the name of our Lord Jesus Christ.

Young parents are always fun to watch. They wait so long for their first baby to come. They wonder what their child will be like, what kind of hair they will have, or whether or not they will be athletic or more cerebral.

Then the big day comes along. Their first child arrives. For a while the baby just sits there, not doing much. I guess that I was like most young dads in that I was shocked when our firstborn daughter just sat there, doing very little. She crawled around the house from time to time but more or less she was sedentary. But then the big day arrived; she got upon her two feet and began to walk. And it is has been downhill since then. Our little bundle of joy was everywhere.

New parents have no idea of the energy involved in watching a walking child. They get into everything as they explore the world around them. Children climb up the stairs and down the stairs, into the kitchen and out of the kitchen, in the playroom and out of the playroom. They are exploring their world on their own terms and on their own time. They learn boundaries and rules. Parents have to keep a watchful eye out for these young ones or else they might hurt themselves. They are too young, of course, to stay out of trouble. No parent worth their salt is going to allow their little girl or boy to walk into the street by themselves. Parents usually say things like, "Don't go there, go here" or "Don't go into the kitchen, stay in the play room." We have to watch our children constantly so that they do not get into trouble or hurt themselves. A house after all can be a dangerous place.

And it is sometimes frustrating too because as parents we are not always sure that we are doing the right thing; we are new at this. So much of raising a child is trial and error. A good friend of mine confessed to me one day that if God wanted us to have a how-to manual to raise children, he would have given us one in the first place. Sometimes I wish he did! But God cares for us more than we think he does, and actually he does give us a manual about life. It does not necessarily give us all the details about living but it does offer us a framework or a boundary on which our life is lived. The Bible is our manual. The Bible, God's Word, shapes and forms us and gives us boundaries on how we live out our life of faith. It doesn't give us all the answers, nor does it give us a lot of details; we have to figure a lot out on our own. But the Bible is a good place to start.

Paul was very much like a father to the Ephesians; he brought them the good news of Jesus, staying in this large city for quite some time. He instructed them about living a Christian life in this world. Paul loved the Ephesians just like a parent loves their child. He cared for them very much so he sent a letter warning them about the trials and tribulations, and the various things that they might encounter in their new life in Christ. He wanted them to follow the Lord, not the whims and ways of the world.

Yet Paul was not the first one to talk about walking. In the book of Genesis there is a beautiful passage that says that on one day after creation that Adam and Eve walked with God in the cool of the day. What a beautiful image to have, that God walked with his new creatures side by side, showing them around Paradise. I imagine God walking and talking about the different plants, animals, birds, guiding Adam and Eve through the dense forests and trees and flowers, and over the streams and rivers. Yet Adam and Eve didn't stay in Paradise long. They basically thumbed their nose at God and slammed the door like a teenager. God said, fine, and out they went into the big bold world, experiencing their life and as the author of Genesis says, they had to earn their bread from the sweat of their brow. The psalms and proverbs also speak about walking with God, walking in his law and his commandments. Walking in his ways. Walking in light and truth.

I guess we are very much like Adam and Eve sometimes, trying to make it on our own, like toddlers and teenagers. We want to explore the world in all its finery and beauty. And as teenagers we want to do it on our own, without anyone's help. We are good at saying "No, I don't need you." Yet God still calls us and hopefully we respond. We hear his voice and we follow.

I put my young daughter in the playroom and I walked halfway across the house and went into the kitchen. A wall separates our kitchen from the playroom so she couldn't see me. I called her name and waited. And I called her name again. My daughter crawled all the way across the house to find me. She trusted her hearing rather than her sight and she followed me halfway across the house.

God is always calling us to be with him and we follow him. It is not an easy task, but the Bible refers to his followers as children, and children we are. Sometimes we are like spoiled children trying to live life on our own without him. We usually wander off the path, getting lost and sometimes getting into trouble. But God never gives up on his children. He keeps calling our names hoping that we put our trust in him, and search him out among all the different voices in the world.

Food for Thought

1. Have you ever wandered off the path and lost touch with God? Have you fallen away from faith? How did you return back to God?

2. We cannot live alone, God created us for community. The famous Catholic writer and monk Thomas Merton wrote a book, which he titled *No Man Is an Island*. We might be individuals but we are all connected to one another through our common humanity, and in the Church through our baptism, confirmation, and participation in the other sacraments. How can we create wholesome communities where we live today?

3. Take some time today and pray for those who have lost their way.

4. For further reading: Genesis 1; Jonah 1; Colossians 3:18—4:1

Day 28

He Was Known to Them in the Breaking of the Bread
Luke 24:18–35

As they came near the village to which they were going, he walked ahead as if he were going on. But they urged him

*strongly, saying, "Stay with us, because it is almost evening
and the day is now nearly over." So he went in to stay with
them. When he was at the table with them, he took bread,
blessed and broke it, and gave it to them. Then their eyes were
opened, and they recognized him; and he vanished from their
sight. They said to each other, "Were not our hearts burning
within us while he was talking to us on the road, while he was
opening the scriptures to us?" That same hour they got up and
returned to Jerusalem; and they found the eleven and their
companions gathered together. They were saying, "The Lord
has risen indeed, and he has appeared to Simon!" Then they
told what had happened on the road, and how he had been made
known to them in the breaking of the bread.*

I love to cook. Whenever I have a free moment, I am in
the kitchen creating a new dish or preparing a meal.
Cooking is very therapeutic for me. Chopping and dicing
peppers for a stir-fry, waiting for a sauce to simmer, or
preparing a salad puts me in touch with the basics of life.
After all, we all need food to survive. Some people think
cooking is a chore; I look at it as cocreating with God, making something out of nothing as we read in Genesis, "Then
God said, 'Let there be light'; and there was light" (Gen 1:3).

I like cooking, but *I love baking*. There is nothing better than taking basic materials like yeast, flour, salt, and
egg and combining them in different ways to make bread.
I am not talking about the kind of bread for the bread
machine, I am talking about making a good old-fashioned
batch of bread, where you mix a lot of dough, let it rise,
punch it down, form four or five loaves, and put them in
the oven. I am talking French baguettes, eight-grain bread,
white sandwich bread, cinnamon-raisin bread, and

banana bread. There is nothing better than to come home to the smell of freshly baked bread cooling on the counter, and then spreading a smattering of butter and jam on it and sitting down with a hot cup of coffee and eating it. What more can one ask for in life?

Bread is a staple found throughout the world—yeast breads, flat breads, and everything in between. Arabs have pita, flat bread that is used to scoop up hummus and baba ghanoush. French have *boules* and baguettes, which go great with cheese and apples, and of course wine. Northern Europeans have large, hard, crusty wheat breads that look like cinder blocks. I always thought that you could kill someone with a loaf of that bread! No matter where I travel I always notice what type of bread people are eating.

Bread is very important in the Bible, too. In the Exodus story the Israelites were in such a hurry that God told them, Don't even worry about letting the bread rise in the ovens. Pharaoh was coming and they had to high-tail it out of Egypt. Now they eat unleavened bread at every Passover in remembrance of God's salvation. God must have a sense of humor because he sent them some funny bread called manna. The Bible says that it looked like white frost on the ground. Whatever it was, they didn't like the manna too much since the Israelites started to grumble against God; they were looking for something else to eat. Then in the New Testament we know that Jesus liked bread too since he multiplied the five loaves and the two fish and fed the five thousand men, women, and children. Now that's a lot of bread.

Luke tells us after Jesus' death on the cross his disciples were walking to the village of Emmaus, which was about seven miles from Jerusalem. They must have been quite distraught since their master and teacher was dead. They watched attentively as Jesus was beaten, scourged, ridiculed, spat upon, and hung on the cross to die. They had to flee Jerusalem in fear. Now what were they going to do? Who was going to lead them? Who was going to teach them?

As they were walking to Emmaus, a man came to them inquiring what had happened. Then this man, who was actually the risen Lord, told them everything from Moses and the prophets referred to Jesus. Then Jesus took bread, blessed it, broke it, and gave it to the disciples, and Luke reports that, "then their eyes were opened, and they recognized him; and he vanished from their sight." At the end of the passage the disciples report back to the other disciples: "Then they told what had happened on the road, and how he had been made known to them in the breaking of the bread" (Luke 24:35).

Jesus was known to them in the breaking of the bread! Wow, what good news! This is the good news of the resurrection, retold by Jesus to his disciples, and by his disciples to the ends of the world. After Jesus' resurrection he sent out his disciples into the world so that they could proclaim this good news. We have several examples of this in the Book of Acts where the first Christians tended to the scriptures, the prayers, and the breaking of the bread:

Awe came upon everyone, because many wonders and signs were being done by the apostles. All who believed were together and had all things in common; they would sell their possessions and goods and distribute the proceeds to all, as any had need. Day by day, as they spent much time together in the temple, they broke bread at home and ate their food with glad and generous hearts, praising God and having the goodwill of all the people. And day by day the Lord added to their number those who were being saved. (Acts 2:43–48)

After he had said this, he took bread; and giving thanks to God in the presence of all, he broke it and began to eat. Then all of them were encouraged and took food for themselves. (We were in all two hundred and seventy-six persons in the ship.) After they had satisfied their hunger, they lightened the ship by throwing the wheat into the sea. (Acts 27:35–38)

These two passages from Acts show us that the first Christians maintained the custom of the baking of the bread as part of their regular time together. It was in this context of table fellowship where they gathered together to recall the works and deeds of Jesus and to share this common love, what we often refer to as *agape*, in the breaking of the bread. In our sacramental language, we refer to this as the Eucharist, the giving of thanks. When Christians gather together on Sunday for Mass and the Eucharist, we remember everything that the Lord has done for us. We read from the scriptures, hear a sermon by the pastor or priest that hopefully makes the Bible come alive for us in our daily life, and then we break bread, following the command of the Lord at his Last Supper, " 'Take, eat; this is my body.' Then he took a cup, and after giving thanks he gave it to them, saying, 'Drink from it, all of you; for this is my blood of the covenant, which is poured out for many for the forgiveness of sins'" (Matt 26:26–29). Every Sunday we partake of Jesus' broken body and spilled blood, which feeds and nourishes us, a sign of our fellowship with him and with the rest of the Body of Christ, the Church. Every Sunday we are recommitting ourselves to Christ and the Church, to try to follow him the best that we can and to perform acts of mercy. This is not always easy but we strive to do the best that we can. The following week we once again return to Church and do the same thing, breaking bread and seeing the risen Lord!

Food for Thought

1. Jesus took simple things in life such as bread and wine and told us to remember him when we eat them. We do this on Sunday at communion. However, have you thought of your lunch or dinner as a mini-Eucharist or Thanksgiving? Every time we break bread we are giving thanks to God.

2. We consume all types of food every day, but do we take the time to recall all of the people who work hard to grow, sell, and produce that food for our consumption? I love coffee and once in a while I stop and think of the farmers in Costa Rica and Brazil who plant and harvest the coffee beans. Then there is the wholesaler who packages and ships the coffee to the United States. Then there is the local coffee shop that purchases the coffee and sells it. So many people are involved in feeding us. Take some time out of your day

and thank God for the people who bring us food each and every day.

3. In John 6, Jesus refers to himself as the bread of life. How is Jesus our bread? In what ways does he feed us? How can we share this bread, meaning Jesus, with other people?

4. For further reading: Exodus 16; 1 Kings 17:8–16; Matthew 14:13–21

Day 29

Catching the Spirit
Acts 2:1–4

When the day of Pentecost had come, they were all together in one place. And suddenly from heaven there came a sound like the rush of a violent wind, and it filled the entire house where they were sitting. Divided tongues, as of fire, appeared among them, and a tongue rested on each of them. All of them were filled with the Holy Spirit and began to speak in other languages, as the Spirit gave them ability.

Fire is such an important thing in our life. It gives light, helps us cook our food, and provides warmth. I cannot imagine life without fire. Our congregation uses beeswax candles, and I enjoy sitting in Church sometimes and watching parishioners light their candles. They take the light from one candle and pass it on to light another one. One candle lighting another. Too much fire, of course, is not good. We have all heard of terrible tragedies when a house burns down or a chemical fire burns for days. Once in a while you even hear of a polluted lake or river catching on fire because of the toxic chemicals that are continuously being dumped.

At Pentecost, tongues of fire rested on each of the apostles. The apostles were gathered together in the Upper Room in Jerusalem in order to celebrate the Jewish feast of Pentecost that commemorates the giving of the Ten Commandments to Moses. Pentecost is also referred to as the birthday of the Church since it is on the feast of Pentecost when the apostles went forth preaching and teaching the gospel, baptizing new Christian believers, and establishing the Church of Christ.

The crowds thought that Peter and the other disciples were drunk because, after all, it was early in the day and they were speaking in foreign tongues and acting very strange. However, Peter and the other disciples were not drunk as people supposed they were but instead were full of the Holy Spirit. They began to speak in different tongues, preaching in the various languages of the Roman Empire, which are listed in the previous gospel passage: Parthians, Medes, Elamites, residents of Cappadocia, Pontus, and Asia (Acts 2:9). In other words, everyone heard the gospel being preached in their own native tongue. The feast of Pentecost is a feast of preaching; the apostles, filled with the Holy Spirit, received the gift of proclaiming the gospel to the whole world. Everyone in

Jerusalem heard the gospel being preached in their own language, a very strange act.

These gifts of tongues are referred to as being tongues of fire, which is a reference to a passage in the Gospel of Luke where John the Baptist says that while he baptizes with water, Jesus will baptize with the Holy Spirit and with fire. John answered all of them by saying, "I baptize you with water; but one who is more powerful than I is coming; I am not worthy to untie the thong of his sandals. He will baptize you with the Holy Spirit and fire" (Luke 3:16). It is important to note that the gift of speech that the disciples had was understood by those around them. In other words the disciples were not speaking in some incomprehensible, mumbo-jumbo but in words that people could understand. Paul, of course, emphasizes this notion of understanding in his Epistle to the Corinthians.

For us, every Pentecost is a commemoration of that first outpouring of the Holy Spirit on the Church and Jesus' commands to his disciples that they continue in his preaching and teaching ministry until he comes again. At Pentecost we are encouraged to reaffirm again our baptismal calling to live according to the Word of God and proclaim it the best we can, in both our words and our deeds as we are witnesses to the death and resurrection of Jesus.

In many ways our baptism and confirmation in the Church are each a mini-Pentecost, a time when we are given a little dose of the Holy Spirit in life. When we receive the body and blood of Christ we are receiving the gift of the Holy Spirit as well. This is very important because we cannot remain complacent in our faith. When the disciples received the tongues of fire, they reacted by going out of Jerusalem and spreading the good news to the rest of the world. When the Apostle Paul was baptized by Ananias, he also received the Holy Spirit and became one of the most important preachers of the gospel.

When *we* receive the Holy Spirit, the fire of the Spirit ignites us. We are called to react to it! The question is, How will we react? How can we better live a life of faith in this world? How can we be more faithful disciples of Christ? How can we pass on this faith to our children and to our grandchildren? How can we be ambassadors of the Church to our family, friends, and neighbors? Each one of us will have a different answer and a different way to accomplish such acts. No two people are alike. We all have different families and live in different situations. However, we are all Christians who have received the great gift of the Holy Spirit and need to share that gift with others. So what are you waiting for? Go out and start today!

Food for Thought

1. Pentecost is a time for spiritual renewal when the Church is renewed by the Spirit of God for works of mercy, compassion, and forgiveness. How can you contribute to this renewal in your parish community, in your neighborhood, and in your family?

2. When I was a child, I used to sing the song "This Little Light of Mine." The song speaks of sharing our light with one another. How can you share the light of Christ with the people

around you? Every day we have a choice to let our light shine or not to shine—it is really up to us!

3. For further reading: Leviticus 23:15–21; Isaiah 5:24; Joel 2:28–33; John 20:19–23

DAY 30

Angels We Have Heard on High
LUKE 1:26–38

In the sixth month the angel Gabriel was sent by God to a town in Galilee called Nazareth, to a virgin engaged to a man whose name was Joseph, of the house of David. The virgin's name was Mary. And he came to her and said, "Greetings, favored one! The Lord is with you." But she was much perplexed by his words and pondered what sort of greeting this might be. The angel said to her, "Do not be afraid, Mary, for you have found favor with God. And now, you will conceive in your womb and bear a son, and you will name him Jesus. He will be great, and will be called the Son of the Most High, and the Lord God will give to him the throne of his ancestor David. He will reign over the house of Jacob for ever, and of his kingdom there will be no end."

I have never seen an angel in real life, only on television shows like *Touched by An Angel*, with Della Reese and Roma Downey. I have seen angels on plenty of greeting cards and wallpaper; you know, those cute little cherubs floating on clouds while playing their harps and blowing their trumpets. They seem so cute and benign. However, the Bible tells us that angels are not that cute and certainly not very benign.

Nine months before the birth of Jesus, the angel Gabriel came to Mary and told her that she was going to bear the Son of God. "And he came to her and said, 'Greetings, favored one! The Lord is with you.' But she was much perplexed and pondered what sort of greeting this might be. And the angel said to her, 'Do not be afraid, Mary, for you have found favor with God. And behold, you will conceive in your womb and bear a son, and you shall call his name Jesus' " (Luke 1:26–31). Luke continues by telling us that Mary accepted this invitation and pondered these words in her heart. This annunciation story is a familiar one and has been the subject for numerous works of art, poetry, and song. Yet one may ask, Why was Mary afraid of an angel if he was bringing her good news from God?

Angels are mentioned throughout the scriptures and are known as God's messengers. In the Book of Genesis an angel of the Lord wrestles with Jacob. After a long battle that lasted until the next morning, Jacob loses and his name is changed from Jacob to Israel (Gen 28:10–17). An angel also approaches the prophet Isaiah and touches Isaiah's lips with a burning coal because he is a sinner (Isa 6:7). An angel comes to Joseph and reassures him not to divorce Mary but to care for her and her newborn child (Matt 1:18–25). An angel appears to the myrrh-bearing women as they approach the tomb on the first Easter Sunday and tells them to go tell the disciples that Jesus is risen from the dead. Likewise, angels appear in the Book of Revelation — thousands and ten thousands.

Gabriel's message might seem benign. Every year during this feast we hear this gospel and we see the iconographic image of the annunciation on many Christmas cards and in Churches. However, if we take this message in the context and background of the first century, we realize its power. We have to remember that during the time when Jesus was born, most of what we consider to be the Middle East was under the power and authority of the Roman Empire, specifically under the guidance and leadership of Augustus Caesar.

Knowing this background gives us a better understanding of the annunciation to Mary. Gabriel's message to Mary is awesome if we realize that Augustus Caesar ruled the empire and that the Roman government and military were strong; yet Mary's son Jesus would be true king with the ultimate power and authority in the world.

Mary's responds to Gabriel in the following manner: "How can this be, since I am a virgin?" (Luke 1:34). Mary's question is very ordinary; after all, how can a virgin bear a child? However, Gabriel reminds Mary that with God all things are possible. If God made the heavens and the earth, parted the Red Sea to allow the Israelites to pass through, if he fed the Israelites the manna from heaven, he can also allow the virgin birth! He is the God who is now working through Mary in order to bring a savior, a new Joshua who will save us from our sins!

Food for Thought

1. The Virgin Mary heard Gabriel's message and said yes to God. Her yes allowed the Son of God to be born. Could you imagine what the world would be like if she said no! What a terrible thought that she would have said no to God. Mary was a chosen vessel and for her we give thanks to God. Take some time out of your hectic week and think about Mary and what she did for humanity. Think about her conceiving the Christ Child, giving birth to Jesus, raising Jesus, and finally watching her son die on the cross.

2. Mary has a very special place in the scriptures and in our spirituality. She is referred to by some Christians as the Queen of Heaven, the Mediatrix, and the Queen of Peace. There are special feast days held in her honor such as the annunciation and her assumption. And some Christians remember Mary by reciting the Rosary.

3. For further reading: Genesis 28:10–17; 1 Samuel 2:1–10; Luke 1:46–55

Appendix

Lectio Divina
A Way of Reading Scripture

It is tempting to read the scriptures quickly and then move on to the rest of our daily activities. We live in such a fast-paced world that even as we sit down and begin reading a passage from the Bible, a thousand thoughts may cross our mind. What do I have to do later today? What time is my lunch meeting? Who will pick up the kids from school? Where is my to-do list that I wrote this morning? How can I ever make it through this hectic day? We get distracted by so many thoughts that if we are not careful, we can miss the message of whatever scripture lesson we are reading. Therefore, we need to take ample time and slowly read each passage, think about what we are reading, and then ask ourselves: How can this scripture passage be understood or applied in my life today? What is God saying to me now? What difference can these words make in my life? When reading the Bible slowly, we allow the words to run over us like water running over our head, slowly seeping into our very skin and bones. So too, we read the Bible in a slow way, allowing the words to flow across our minds and hearts.

This method of slow meditative reading, called *lectio divina*, or "divine reading," has been practiced by Christians for centuries. *Lectio divina*, or simply *lectio*, is a slow, meditative way of reading scripture in which the reader ruminates or actually chews on each word, considers what the word means, and explores how it connects to the rest of the scriptures. *Lectio* takes time and cannot be rushed.

Practicing *lectio divina* requires that you take a few moments out of your busy schedule and find a quiet place at home, at work, or somewhere outside such as a park bench. Remove yourself from all distractions; you can even close your eyes for a few moments, but make sure you don't fall asleep! Then open your Bible and read a few passages from scripture. It is important to keep in mind that reading less is more. The aim of *lectio* is to allow the Word of God to permeate our minds and our hearts. It is better to have a good understanding of a few verses in the Bible than to read a few chapters and have no idea what you are reading. For example, let's imagine that you begin reading the first few verses of Psalm 23:

> The LORD is my shepherd I shall not want.
> He makes me lie down in green pastures;
> he leads me beside still waters;
> he restores my soul.
> He leads me in paths of righteousness
> for his name's sake.
>
> Even though I walk through the valley of the shadow
> of death
> I fear no evil;
> for thou art with me;
> Thy rod and thy staff—
> they comfort me.

When reading slowly, take in every word as it comes to you. Read the first verse, "The Lord is my shepherd." What does it mean that the Lord is described as a shepherd? How is the Lord *your* shepherd? If the Lord is described as a shepherd, this means that we are his sheep. How are we like sheep? Do we always follow him where he leads us? Are we always obedient to his every command? Likewise, how does God restore my weary soul in times of doubt or distress? In the ancient Near East, a shepherd led his sheep out from the desert areas and into the lush green valleys near streams and rivers so that the sheep could find food and water. He would walk in front of them with his staff while at the same time making sounds with his mouth or with a bell so that the sheep would know where he was. If a few sheep were hanging at the back of the herd, the shepherd would go and get them. He led them across small streams, slept outside with them in the evening, and brought them to dry ground during inclement weather. In other words, a shepherd was totally committed to taking care of his sheep. Therefore, after reading just a few verses from Psalm 23 and learning the importance of the shepherd in the ancient world, we begin to see how God is our shepherd, taking care of our needs, giving us what we need when we need it. When we take time to read slowly, we will begin to appreciate the words of the Bible more deeply.

If we begin reading the scriptures with *lectio* in mind, we will begin to unlock the vast meaning of the words on the page which will then come to life for us. However, you will also find that when practicing *lectio* you will return to God's Word again and again throughout the day. As you walk your dog in the evening, you may remember that the Lord is your shepherd. While driving to work in the morning, you might think about the Lord leading you to the still waters, and no matter what happens with that big decision that you have to make at work, you will be okay with the results. Later at home in the evening, you might recall that as a sheep you need to listen to God's voice throughout the daytime, reflecting on your life in terms of your work, family, friends, and Church. Thus, practicing *lectio* allows God's Word to permeate and fill us with the good news with the intent of establishing good roots in the fertile soils of our minds and hearts, hopefully producing fruits of repentance.

Recommended Reading

Bianchi, Enzo. *Praying the Word: An Introduction to Lectio Divina*. Kalamazoo, MI: Cistercian Publications, 1998.
———. *Words of the Inner Life*. Toronto: Novalis, 2002.
Brown, Raymond E. *Christ in the Gospels of the Liturgical Year (Expanded Edition With Essays)*. Collegeville, MN: The Liturgical Press, 2008.
Johnson, Luke Timothy. *Living Jesus: Learning the Heart of the Gospel*. San Fransisco: Harper Collins, 1999.
Louf, Andre. *Tuning In to Grace: The Quest for God*. Kalamazoo, MI: Cistercian Publications, 1992.
Martin, James. *Becoming Who You Are*. Mahwah, NJ: HiddenSpring Books, 2006.
Mills, William C. *Our Father: A Prayer for Christian Living*. Rollinsford, NH: Orthodox Research Institute, 2008.
Norris, Kathleen. *Amazing Grace: A Vocabulary of Faith*. New York: Riverhead, 1998.
O' Collins, Gerard. *Following the Way: Jesus, Our Spiritual Director*. Mahwah, NJ: Paulist Press, 2001.
Watson, William. *Inviting God into Your Life*. Mahwah, NJ: Paulist Press, 2003.
Williams, Rowan. *Where God Happens: Discovering Christ in One Another*. Boston: MA: New Seeds, 2005.
Wills, Gary. *What Jesus Meant*. New York: Viking, 2006.
———. *What Paul Meant*. New York: Viking, 2007.
———. *What the Gospels Meant*. New York: Viking, 2008.

green press
INITIATIVE

Paulist Press is committed to preserving ancient forests and natural resources. We elected to print this title on 30% post consumer recycled paper, processed chlorine free. As a result, for this printing, we have saved:

4 Trees (40' tall and 6-8" diameter)
1 Million BTUs of Total Energy
333 Pounds of Greenhouse Gases
1,605 Gallons of Wastewater
97 Pounds of Solid Waste

Paulist Press made this paper choice because our printer, Thomson-Shore, Inc., is a member of Green Press Initiative, a nonprofit program dedicated to supporting authors, publishers, and suppliers in their efforts to reduce their use of fiber obtained from endangered forests.

For more information, visit www.greenpressinitiative.org

Environmental impact estimates were made using the Environmental Defense Paper Calculator. For more information visit: www.papercalculator.org.